*How to Get Into
and Finance Graduate
and Professional Schools*

A Step-by-Step Guide for Current and Returning Students

COLLIER BOOKS
A Division of Macmillan Publishing Co., Inc.
NEW YORK

HOW TO GET INTO AND FINANCE GRADUATE AND PROFESSIONAL SCHOOLS

STEPHEN J. WILLIAMS

Copyright © 1982 by Stephen J. Williams

All rights reserved. No part of this book may be reproduced or transmitted in any form or by any means, electronic or mechanical, including photocopying, recording or by any information storage and retrieval system, without permission in writing from the Publisher.

Macmillan Publishing Co., Inc.
866 Third Avenue, New York, N.Y. 10022
Collier Macmillan Canada, Inc.

Library of Congress Cataloging in Publication Data

Williams, Stephen Joseph, 1948–
    How to get into and finance graduate and professional schools.

        Includes index.
        1. Universities and colleges—United States—Graduate work. 2. Universities and colleges—United States—Admission. 3. Universities and colleges—United States—Graduate work—Finance. I. Title.
LB2371.W47   1982   378'.1553'0973   82–17701
ISBN 0-02-015940-4

---

10 9 8 7 6 5 4 3 2 1

Printed in the United States of America

For Sandra and Jeffrey

Contents

	Preface	ix
	PART I BEFORE YOU APPLY	
Chapter 1	The Admissions Process	3
Chapter 2	Relating Career Goals to Application Processes	11
Chapter 3	Choosing the School	20
Chapter 4	Initiating Contact with Your Future School	29
	PART II MAKING APPLICATION	
Chapter 5	Completing the Application Forms	37
Chapter 6	References and Other Testimonials to Your Potential	52
Chapter 7	Quantitative Data on Your Past: Prior Training and Grades	66
Chapter 8	Coping with Standardized Tests	83
Chapter 9	Your Experience and Background	95
Chapter 10	The Interview and How to Handle It	102

PART III SPECIAL SITUATIONS

Chapter 11	Using Connections and Back-Door Admissions	129
Chapter 12	Women and Minorities	139
Chapter 13	The Decisions, and How to Cope	149
Chapter 14	What to Do If You're Rejected	161

PART IV FINANCING YOUR EDUCATION

Chapter 15	Financing Your Education: Practical Considerations	169
Chapter 16	Financing Your Education: Sources of Funds	190

PART V READY TO ACT

Chapter 17	Formulating Your Strategies	215

APPENDIXES

Appendix A	Personal Assessment Table	221
Appendix B	Financial-Aid Worksheet for Graduate and Professional Students	226
Appendix C	A Glossary of Admissions and Financial-Aid Terms	229
	Index	233
	About the Author	240

Preface

To A REMARKABLE NUMBER of aspiring students, the process of applying for admission to graduate and professional programs constitutes a mysterious and strange ritual. They submit themselves and their future destinies quite willingly to a process of which they have little knowledge and over which they have almost no control. For the schools there is a parallel apprehension about the potential student, whom they often know only on paper, yet with whom they may be "living" for many years. This is an unfortunate state of affairs for everyone.

The process of applying to graduate and professional schools consists of much more than just completing forms and taking admissions tests. It is the culmination of years of thought and preparation, many hours of frustration and concern, and sometimes the result of pressures from family, friends, and the student's own desires to succeed. It is also the beginning of a new period in a person's life.

For society and for the schools, admissions also represents the critical point at which the selection of the nation's future doctors, lawyers, business leaders, and other professionals occurs. You, the applicant, are not only applying to a school, you are seeking to enter a profession. Thus the selection process means much more than deciding which bright and eager students will be showing up at the school's front door the following fall. The admissions process, then, is very critical both for our nation and for your chosen profession. And in many fields, such as law or medicine, completion of graduate or professional education is the only way you can become a member of the "fraternity" of practitioners.

For you personally graduate and professional education also should be more than a way to stay off the streets for a few more years. You have reached a critical decision point in your life. Few current or recent graduate students would recommend that you take lightly the financial sacrifices and years of hard work that are involved unless you are reasonably committed to your new career. There may be a few geniuses, like Michael Crichton, who go through medical school and then become best-selling writers without ever practicing medicine full-time, but most people will not want to spend years of effort and expense training for one field only to devote their life to other interests. And since there are few fields for which there are enough good training opportunities for all who apply, your inappropriate choice of a field may deny a place to someone who is more committed. Worse still, the feeling of obligation to carry through after years of arduous training may lead you into a lifetime of work in a field in which you are not really happy or satisfied. And the financial and emotional costs of training may exceed the benefits you eventually achieve as a professional.

The primary purposes of this book are to help you improve your chances of admission to graduate and professional programs and to assist you in identifying the costs of, and sources of support for, your education. But there is a broader message in this book than just the nuances and quirks of the admissions and financial-aid processes. That message is that success in graduate and professional schools, and in the world of practice that follows, is a result of many complex factors. Part of that success, and part of the success that you will have in gaining admission and identifying sources of support, depends on the extent to which you have completely thought through your own career goals.

Preface

The decisions that are made by admissions and financial-aid committees involve much more than just your individual credentials. They are decisions not just of who is to be admitted to next fall's class, but also of who will be admitted to the field of practice. If you think in these terms, you will understand better how admissions processes work, how the decisions are made, and, in the final analysis, how to improve your chances of gaining admission. In many instances the same logic and thought processes also apply to financial aid.

This book presents the individual factors involved in admissions and financial aid. But there is a word of warning necessary in following such an approach, especially with respect to admissions. The decision about whom to admit, which is the bottom line to you as an applicant, is the synergistic result of all of the various components of the admissions process. Following a belief that you can improve your chances of admission by improving your credentials in each component, advice is offered category by category. However, admissions decisions are often the result of trading off an applicant's attributes in the different categories. Thus, if you face limits in how well you can present yourself in any one category, such as grades or test scores, remember that by standing out elsewhere you can at least partially compensate for deficiencies in these other areas.

Also keep in mind that applying to graduate and professional schools for admission and financial aid is essentially a mechanical effort that is completed in a relatively short time. And in spite of all of the forms and tests and other hoops that you have to jump through, it is a process that takes relatively little effort. On the other hand, much of the information that you will be presenting has been accumulated over a period of many years. While this book will tell you how to compensate for some of your past errors, you should recognize that individuals who spent their college years with the single-minded purpose of gaining admission to graduate or professional programs have an advantage. The wisest applicants will be reading this book during their freshman or sophomore years in college, when there are still opportunities for improving grades, gaining practical work experience, and otherwise accumulating an impressive track record.

If you are reading these words and are thinking back to your glorious, fun-filled academic years, notable for your less than stellar academic performance, don't despair. This book is also designed to help you attempt to overcome those earlier "deficiencies."

But every applicant should remember that no one can erase their record. Your credentials will all be reviewed and assessed by the admissions and financial-aid committees. Do not be misled by the rumor that committees ignore the first two or three years of college. As any good parent will tell you, hard work and fruitful study in college pays off much better than adventure and play, at least in terms of professional development.

If you are reading this book and squirming, your best bet is to read the chapters that follow very carefully and to stress your finest attributes. Also, you might advise your younger friends and relatives to read this book at an earlier point in their career than you have done. If you are reading this book and smirking because you have thought ahead about graduate and professional study and are confident that you will have a leg up on your happy-go-lucky classmates, remember that a lot happens before the final decision is reached. You still have a long path to travel, and you must become aware of the potential hazards and roadblocks that could deter you from reaching your goal. Each year many highly qualified applicants receive rejection letters they never dreamed they would receive; it can happen to you if you are careless.

There are hundreds of graduate and professional fields. For the most part the admissions processes are similar in all fields, and, frankly, many of the standards and criteria used for admission decisions are also similar. Virtually every school seeks the most qualified, brightest, most honest, and most capable students that they can possibly attract. Most look at the same or a similar set of credentials. As a result, many aspects of admissions and financial-aid activities can be discussed from a "generic" point of view. Thus, many of the ways in which you can improve your chances of admission or of financial aid are similar regardless of which type of school or program you are applying to. Many of the tricks of the trade that will be discussed in this book apply to virtually all schools. For most fields of study the information provided in this book will go a long way toward helping you understand the admissions process, improve your chances of gaining acceptance, and think in the context of your long-term career goals.

Finally, there are no shortcuts. Read through the chapters, make notes, study the suggestions, outline your own qualifications, and list your personal strengths and weaknesses. Follow through on suggestions for accentuating strengths and compensating for your weaknesses.

Do not lie to yourself or misrepresent yourself to the admissions committee. You can improve your situation without misrepresentation. Most admissions committees can see through misrepresentation—they have seen it before and know most of the tricks that applicants have tried over the years. Present yourself in the best possible light, but in a realistic and honest way.

The advice presented in the following chapters should be of immense value to you. However, be aware that there are many additional sources of free information that are available to you. Be persistent and seek out such advice and assistance where you feel it might be useful. The better prepared you are to answer your own questions about where you have been, where you are going, and what you are all about, the better you will be able to impress and inform the admissions committee.

By now you should be relatively convinced that there is a lot more to the admissions process than filling out a series of forms. It is a complex activity that involves much more than the mechanical actions apparent on the surface. If you understand that alone, you have already gained valuable advice from your brief expenditure of time reading this book. You have begun to open the black boxes that the admissions and financial-aid processes often appear to be to the applicant. And you will have begun to understand the psychology of the people who make the decisions. You will see that these people take admissions and financial aid very seriously for some very good reasons.

A lot of time is spent on admissions and on financial aid by the many applicants who seek entry to graduate and professional schools each year. But you would probably be surprised by the huge commitments of time and effort that the schools allocate for admissions and by the many heated debates that are held each year over individual applicants' credentials and, more importantly, over the standards and criteria used for admissions decisions.

The final admonition is very personal. You must, in reading this book, in applying to graduate and professional schools, and in financing your education, think of yourself first and foremost. This book will reveal to you the workings of the admissions process and how to improve your opportunities for financial aid. You must reveal to yourself your own personal goals, your attributes and weaknesses, and your motivations. You must think not just in terms of which schools you can get into, but rather in terms of which career goals are the best for you and how you can achieve those goals.

Don't despair. These are not easy choices for you, and rest assured that they are equally hard choices for the people making the admissions decisions. Contrary to what you may think, many faculty are disturbed by how hard it is to select among qualified applicants, about whether the most relevant criteria are being used, and about whether there are biases and prejudices introduced that are inappropriate.

As much as you may feel at the mercy of unknown people who are making decisions about your life, and who may not appear to be acting in your best interest, recognize the complexities of the situation and the competing demands placed on everyone involved. Above all, take the entire process as seriously as the admissions committees and faculty do. You will be surprised at how much such an attitude can pay off for you.

PART I *Before You Apply*

CHAPTER 1 *The Admissions Process*

THE BEST PLACE to begin advising any applicant is with the admissions process, which is far more complex than many applicants realize. You can begin to "psych out" the process only by understanding it better. You should not view it as a black box into which you submit your credentials and out of which comes an acceptance or rejection letter. If you know what is behind the decisions, you are better equipped to act from a position of strength. And while the admissions process varies somewhat from place to place and program to program, it is actually very similar in most instances.

This chapter describes the overall nature and functions of the admissions process. The chapters that follow will look in detail at each step in the process and at the information used to make decisions. Remember, the admissions process is designed to admit people to the profession and is not merely the mechanical review of credentials.

The admissions process is complex, has a number of functions, and should be taken very seriously.

Most faculties spend a lot of time thinking through what they want from the admissions process—types of students that are sought, how to identify them, and even how to attract the right types of applicants. That may not sound too exciting to you if you have been rejected recently, but the fact of the matter is that a lot of effort is put into the admissions process, albeit often to the advantage of the program rather than the applicant.

For the most part you will be dealing with people, all of whom have feelings and biases.

Admissions includes a variety of components, and you should understand the role of each. You would probably be surprised at how many people are involved and how you can inadvertently offend some of them, perhaps reducing your chances of admission. You should also be aware that admissions decisions are made by people, not computers. Computers are used to screen or evaluate applicants, especially when there are large numbers of applicants, but they supplement rather than substitute for humans.

Most important, keep in mind that the faculty members, admissions secretaries, and students with whom you will have contact have feelings, beliefs, biases, and emotions. You can easily offend these people at many points in the admissions process. At the same time you may be able to improve your chances by being appealing to these same people. One of the objectives of this book is to help you understand how to work with these key people. Remember that the admissions process is not the time to assert your independence unless you do so judiciously and carefully. You will want to put the "end result" goals ahead of your need to assert yourself.

You should understand the admissions process from both the applicant's and the school's perspectives.

The admissions process can be viewed from both the school's and the applicant's perspectives. You need to under-

The Admissions Process

stand both. You probably know more about the latter than the former, although you actually know less than you think even about your own perspective. It is important to understand both viewpoints and how they interact. Understanding admissions is a good test of your analytical skills.

You must comply with established routines and provide required information.

From the school's perspective the admissions process has both procedural and substantive aspects. Some needs relate to the handling of reams of paperwork, while others are more germane to the issue of whom to admit. Practically speaking, this means that you must happily comply with the procedural hoops that you are asked to jump through, making available all the information necessary to evaluate your suitability for admission. Since the admissions process requires a lot of effort on the part of the schools, they are not sympathetic to any attempts to shortcut the process, to requests for exemptions from established requirements, or to any individualization of the process to fit one person's needs. The reasons for this are relatively simple and straightforward. The process, and the activities that go on behind the scenes, were established to accomplish a mission on behalf of the faculty—and you should be cognizant that it is the faculty who ultimately have the responsibility for making admissions decisions. While the faculty may delegate some of the admissions duties, they retain the final decision-making authority.

Play along with the established admissions procedures rather than trying to change them.

Since the faculty are busy with many other duties, they usually establish procedures for the accumulation of information and for handling the decision-making referred to as the "admissions process." There is little you can do to change the established processes, and the faculty will not appreciate any attempts to do so.

Treat everyone with whom you come in contact respectfully and pleasantly.

The mechanical aspects of admissions are handled by support staff, secretaries, admissions coordinators, perhaps interviewers, sometimes student workers, and similar people. These individuals have feelings, and you can offend them and thereby perhaps affect your chances of admission, as surprising as that may seem. Be polite to everyone you meet because you can never be sure what their role and influence may be in the admissions process. You might be surprised by how important the support staff is and the extent of their potential influence at times. Of course, in the final analysis be assured that the faculty do in fact make the decisions. But the odd chance of a disparaging comment to a committee member about you is not worth the risk of letting off steam to a secretary or commenting offhandedly that you are above the "Mickey Mouse" procedures you are being forced to comply with.

The admissions process structurally involves more than just the admissions committee, secretary, or staff. It is much more complex and frequently involves a large number of people, only some of whom may actually be directly involved in making decisions. The admissions process is a mechanical manifestation of the faculty's duty to identify and select students. As such, the admissions process must provide all information that the faculty need to make decisions. The admissions decision is an action that is based on the types of students that the faculty feel should be attracted to the program and to the profession. Each applicant's credentials must be compared to criteria and standards that reflect the characteristics of people the faculty seek. Thus the faculty must provide to the admissions committee, which acts on its behalf, a description of acceptable types of students.

The admissions committee acts as an agent of the entire faculty, using criteria and standards that have been established by the faculty to select students.

Since the admissions process is fairly arduous and time-consuming, it is rare that actual decisions are made by all of the faculty. Rather, there is usually a delegation of authority to a selected subset of faculty with the dubious distinction of being members of what is usually termed the "admissions committee." This committee is not a self-appointed group of faculty members who have volunteered to "take care of" admissions.

The relevance of this relatively abstract discussion to the lowly applicant is, first, that the admissions committee is acting on behalf of the entire faculty, to which it is accountable. Admitting all of the committee members' friends and relatives is a violation of that trust and accountability, and would not be tolerated.

Second, since the admissions committee acts on behalf of the entire faculty, the criteria and standards that are applied to individual applicants are not solely the preferences of the committee. Rather, they are in fact the collective wisdom and desires of the entire faculty. The manner in which such desires are communicated to the admissions committee varies greatly. But it would be very rare indeed for the admissions committee to have the authority to establish on its own, without the advice and direction of the rest of the faculty, the criteria for accepting or rejecting applicants. This means that there are limitations on the extent to which the committee can bend the established criteria for your benefit. And the nature of the accountability that is inherent in the selection and appointment of the committee members means that they too must, to an extent, toe the line.

Third, because all faculty are involved in admissions, either by taking turns serving on the admissions committee or by participating in the establishment of criteria and standards for admission, you can find out useful information from people other than those actually serving on the committee at any point in time.

From your perspective the admissions process is an opportunity to present the case for why you should be selected for advanced study. You should recognize that there are not many programs that receive fewer applications than there are entering places available. Every applicant is at some risk of rejection, regardless of how confident one might be. There are many opportunities for an applicant to present information that, in the minds of the admissions committee at least, justifies a rejection. Therefore, all applicants would be wise to present the best case that they possibly can—which is probably part of your reason for purchasing this book.

Analyze each component of the admissions process, and apply the information presented in this book to your situation.

The admissions process must be viewed in terms of its component parts. This includes both the procedural parts and the information-analysis aspects. Since each part of the process can be of critical importance, a separate chapter in this book is devoted to each aspect. Wise applicants will carefully consider the advice presented in the chapters that follow, methodically examining the material presented and applying it to their individual situations.

The admissions process includes opportunities for applicants to present themselves in person, such as contacting the admissions office for information or setting up a personal interview. The process also allows applicants to present to the committee extensive written information, such as grades, test scores, references, and so forth. In some instances there may be considerable leeway for each applicant to determine what is presented, such as in the selection of references or the preparation of a personal statement. The wise applicant will carefully review each part of the process and think through each item of information that is presented. This includes careful selection of references, meticulous preparation of personal statements, and complete preparation of the application forms.

Follow all instructions carefully and completely.

Among the informal ways in which an applicant may be judged is simply the ability to follow instructions. Applications that are poorly prepared or for which important information is missing may reflect a poor attitude or, even worse, a lack of ability to do things right. All of the required procedures must be carefully followed, and all of the required forms and documentation must be submitted. In addition, you should be sensitive to deadlines.

Ultimately, while most applicants can improve their chances for admission by the care with which they apply, some people have such poor credentials that there can be little hope.

Throughout this book you will be provided with information and suggestions that can help you to improve your chances of admission to your desired graduate or professional school. Many of these suggestions are items you may never have even thought of. While there can never be any guarantees about your chances of acceptance, and even relatively minor items can lead to a rejection, diligence in presenting your credentials can improve your chances. Of course, if your grades reflect inept undergraduate performance that, perhaps combined with low test scores or other information, suggests that you are unlikely to succeed in school, there may in fact be little hope for admission regardless of how careful you are. After all, a well-executed application cannot compensate for poor grades or abysmal test scores. But for most applicants there is hope, and for many success may simply require a little polishing of credentials.

The admissions process may be unpleasant to you. Many faculty view it as equally unpleasant for them. Unfortunately, there is no alternative available to match applicants and programs, and for all the imperfections, of which there are many, both applicants and schools remain committed to established admissions procedures and processes. Rather than trying to change the system, you should understand the processes and use them to your advantage by presenting the best possible face to the admissions committee. That is the ultimate purpose of the chapters that follow.

CHAPTER 2 · Relating Career Goals to Application Processes

SUBMITTING AN APPLICATION to a graduate or professional school is the first step in the development of a career that will likely last for many years. You now need to obtain advanced education to enter a chosen field of practice. While most of this book is designed to aid you in improving your chances of admission, and in finding out how to finance your education, this chapter will help you think about the life-style and career implications of your actions.

You will have to have a high level of commitment to complete the program.

Advanced study requires some very serious commitments. First and foremost you will be spending anywhere from one to four or more years of your life in a university, pursuing your studies. While many master's-degree programs are only one or two years long, doctoral programs in such fields as medicine, dentistry, and law are three or four years in length. It is not uncommon for doctoral degrees in many disciplines to require five to seven years of study beyond college. And these will be very long years of not always enjoyable study. Furthermore, in many fields additional years of study are required beyond the formal degree program before one can actually begin to practice. The medical student will complete a residency. The law school graduate will likely initially spend a couple of years in a relatively mundane role in a law firm. A future faculty member may complete a couple of years in a postdoctoral program before assuming a "real" faculty position.

This commitment of time, even if it is "only" a couple of years, must be taken very seriously. Many individuals will forgo what economists term "opportunity costs." These are alternative opportunities you could have pursued during the years you will be in school. The most obvious of these opportunity costs is the income you could have earned if you were working full-time. Another set of opportunity costs relates to career paths that you may pass up during the years of study. For example, a successful career in real estate or business might become an option if you do not proceed with your education. Remember that you will be spending a number of years in the so-called ivory tower, largely isolated from the "real world." This may be frustrating, especially as you watch your friends develop their careers and earn money.

You will have to live on a low income, and this can be especially difficult if you are used to earning a decent wage.

Speaking of money, while you may receive financial aid or have a part-time job, as a full-time student you will still have to live on a very low income. You will spend your time scurrying off to the library to study some obscure topic or to write some seemingly irrelevant paper rather than earning money. Worse yet, you may be forced to use up your savings to pay for your education. Over a period of years the lost income can really add up.

If you are thinking about returning to school after an absence of a few years, you will be in for even more shocks. You are likely to be giving up a lot. You will go from worker and wage-earner to student. Thus, while you will enjoy a certain status that society assigns to graduate and professional students, you will also lose your status as a hardworking, productive, and possibly even successful individual. What's worse, you will lose your income. And unless you are independently wealthy, you will be forced to reduce your standard of living substantially, which can be difficult for even the most frugal of us.

A student is in an often demeaning and unpleasant position in the hierarchy of higher education.

In addition to losing income and status as a working member of society, you will also lose something else. A student is in many ways in a subservient position. While many students like to elevate their status, the reality is somewhat less pleasant —even at the graduate level.

The reality is that, if you are a student in a graduate or professional field, you may be forced to live a relatively demeaning existence. You must complete papers and assignments on time and as instructed by the faculty. You have only limited control over your life. The courses to be completed are often prescribed for you. You have to report for class at a specified time and place. And you are usually treated as one of a number of "products" that the school is turning out.

No amount of personal attention from the faculty can really overcome the basic position in which students find themselves. Many people find this position very unpleasant. And for individuals coming directly from the workplace, who may be used to controlling their own lives, to supervising other people, or even to being the boss, the student role can be downright awful. And there is no "out" short of quitting the program.

Finally, in addition to the mental anguish, the forgone employment opportunities, and the lost income, there is the cost of education itself. Tuition fees, like most everything else in society, have been escalating in recent years. These costs are also a source of concern to the faculty, who want to train only the best and brightest students, especially in publicly supported institutions where tax funds pay for some of the education. Costs of room and board are no less impressive and oppressive. Incidentals such as books and occasional entertainment only add to the burden. Thus there is a direct and often expensive cost associated with advanced training. (The costs of education are discussed further in chapters 15 and 16.)

Graduate education can be difficult, frustrating, and depressing—yet you must maintain your enthusiasm.

The physical and mental burden of advanced study is no small matter. Most graduate and professional programs, especially the better ones, are difficult and not really very enjoyable. The burdens placed on the student are not often recognized or understood. Many parents and friends will simply view you as having a leisurely life walking among the ivy-covered walls of some great university, contemplating the world. This is far from the truth. You will actually be spending long, frustrating, and seemingly nonproductive hours suffering through all types of trauma to achieve one goal: graduation.

Learning can be a remarkably enjoyable experience. You will likely gain knowledge and insight that will be with you for many years and will mark you as a learned person. But you will also complete many assignments that will be boring and may at the time seem irrelevant. No one will appear really to care about you. You may have numerous complaints to lodge against the faculty. You will spend many days and nights pondering whether you have done the right thing, whether this is the path that is best for you. All the while you will have to keep your nose in a book while your friends in the "real world" are having fun and making money.

This rather bleak picture is, of course, somewhat exaggerated. There is a lot of variability in advanced training programs, and the degree to which students face such a dreary existence varies considerably. However, for many students this picture is painfully close to reality. All prospective graduate and professional students must consider if the costs of training are worthwhile.

Graduate and professional education, when taken seriously, requires strong commitment. Even part-time or evening programs, because they are superimposed on a person's private and professional life, require extraordinary commitment and dedication. Every prospective student must weigh the pluses and minuses before proceeding.

Decisions on advanced training should be considered in the context of one's career and personal goals.

The decision over whether to seek advanced training should be placed in a larger context that considers your long-term career and life-development goals. Advanced training is not something that should be sought in the emotions of the moment or in response to what your friends do. In addition to spending more years in school, your entire future career will be determined by this decision. Indeed, your future life-style, perhaps even down to where you end up living, may be determined by these decisions.

This is a turning point in your life. This is a critical time to consider where you want to head in the future. Unfortunately, you may have to make these decisions at an early age. It is not easy to do.

Investigate your own goals as well as the career opportunities that you could pursue.

As you think about applying to graduate or professional school, take the time to analyze your personal goals and objectives in life and how you want to achieve them. This is an ideal time to talk to others, including friends, relatives, and, perhaps most important of all, practitioners in the field that you are thinking about entering. If there are a number of fields that you want to consider, talk to practitioners in each of these areas. Ask hard questions. Ask about the type of life that practitioners live, about the specific types of work performed, about the benefits and rewards, and about the costs involved. These are important questions, and one should not be bashful or hesitant about asking them. Most practitioners will be pleased to tell you about the career opportunities and personal liabilities of their fields.

Do some deep thinking, and ask yourself and others hard personal questions.

Spend time in contemplation and thought. Review your own goals and objectives and what you have discovered about each of the fields you are considering. Talk to counselors or anyone else who can help you sort out your future. It may sound trite, but in future years you may be thankful for the time spent now in thinking through your personal goals in life and deciding on the best avenues for achieving them. You may find that advanced education is not for you or that you want to work for a few years before applying. You may confirm your commitment to school and seek additional training with renewed vigor and enthusiasm. Whatever the results of your efforts, you will be wise to reach a firm conclusion in your own mind before proceeding.

Programs prefer students who have thought out what they want and how additional training fits in.

Since a primary purpose of this book is to help you improve your chances of admission to graduate or professional schools, a few words are in order on the topic of how thinking through your career goals can also help you gain admission. Most graduate and professional programs prefer to accept students who have a clear sense of purpose, who need specific training to achieve their personal goals, and who understand their career objectives.

As discussed in the following chapters, there are a number of ways prospective students can convince the admissions committee that they know where they are going with their lives. These include the personal narrative statement and the interview. The most convincing case can be made by applicants who have thought through their objectives. Thus, spending the time and effort to do this will benefit you not only by clarifying personal and career goals but also by leading to a more convincing application.

Career goals should be thought through and should correlate with the programs to which admission is sought. What education do you need to achieve your personal and career objectives? How can these programs meet your specific educational needs? These are difficult questions to answer, but they must be faced openly and honestly. And the career goals that you outline should be stated in terms of what you actually want to do every day. For example, if you want to deliver babies as a lifetime goal, then you obviously need advanced training as either a physician or a nurse midwife. With a solid rationale for why you want to deliver babies, you can readily justify your need to enter a training program in either medicine or nurse midwifery.

To be frank with yourself, and to present the most carefully thought-out picture to the admissions committee, require detailed planning. Just wanting to "help people" or to "design buildings" is not enough. You should be as specific as your own goals allow. The more decisive you are, up to a point, the more you will appear to understand what you want out of life.

You should have a sense of social commitment.

Most advanced training programs will also be biased toward individuals with some societal commitment. While there is nothing wrong with wanting to make money, it is useful to have some objectives in mind that show a degree of commitment to humanity. However, this commitment should not appear overly naive, too good to be true, or superficial. And you should be realistic with yourself. Pragmatism should be combined with idealism to forge a meaningful personal commitment that will lead you to become a productive member of society.

Take a final step back and be doubly sure that you want to proceed—then fasten your seat belt and read on.

In the final analysis it is the degree to which you have thought out your goals and know where you want to go and how to get there that is perhaps the most important aspect of thinking about further training. Unfortunately, many people look back after years of education and work, and regret having made the career decisions that they did. There is certainly no guarantee that everyone is going to make the best decisions. But that is no reason not to put a lot of effort into trying to make the best possible decision. The admissions committee is likely to perceive whether or not you have thought through what you are doing. And more importantly, you have to live with your decisions.

There is an implicit assumption that you should, in fact, be an applicant. The whole admissions process is really only a mechanical manifestation of a more important societal event, the matching of appropriate individuals to advanced training programs. There are many careers available in our society other than those that require additional years of education.

If the admissions process is something that may not be appropriate for you at this time, then you will be wise to set this book aside, at least temporarily, and do some insightful and contemplative thinking. If, on the other hand, you are ready to plunge ahead, then read on.

CHAPTER 3 *Choosing the School*

CAREFUL SELECTION of the schools to which you apply is of obvious importance in determining your chances of admission. But school selection is even more important from the perspective of your career potential. Many people fail to fully appreciate the degree to which the reputation of the program and the regional and national recognition of the faculty are important to the success of graduating students in finding jobs. Many programs have well-established networks for the communication of information. These are the "old-boy networks," now sometimes broadened to include the "old-girl networks." The extent to which the program, through the faculty, is tied into these networks and is able to communicate with the field of practice will determine at least in part the success of graduates of the program in obtaining initial employment. In some fields, such as medicine, the reputations of the program and its faculty will affect postgraduate training opportunities. Therefore, there is a lot more to choosing a school than simply determining which ones are the easiest to get into. And, of course, there are many other legitimate concerns, such as geographic location, size of classes, availability of various areas of concentration, and so forth, which should be included in your deliberations.

Choosing the School

You should weigh the difficulty of getting into a program against the advantages of attending the more prestigious and selective schools.

The difficulty of getting into a program is often an indication of its reputation and desirability. The more selective the program, usually, the more attractive the job possibilities upon graduation. This is an increasingly important consideration and a practical reason for looking at the difficulty of admission for each program.

Indicators of the selectivity of a program include percentage of applicants accepted, with their median or mean test scores and grade-point averages.

A good indicator of the degree of difficulty of admission for most graduate or professional programs is the percentage of applicants who are accepted. This can be computed by asking the program to provide you with the number of applications received, perhaps for the prior year, and the size of the entering class for the same year. Dividing the latter by the former yields the percentage of applicants accepted. It is also useful to ask if there are any major changes expected in the number of students to be accepted for the year you want to enter or in the anticipated number of applicants.

The information on the percentage of applicants accepted should be combined with the mean or median grade-point averages and standardized test scores for last year's entering class. These measures will provide you with a quantitative measure of the applicant pool's academic abilities as well as an indication of your competitive standing for these criteria.

Collecting this type of information from all of the programs that you are considering should not be very difficult. Most programs are willing to share this information with prospective applicants. They themselves recognize how valuable such information is and are not averse to discouraging applications from people who lack the minimum academic credentials to be seriously considered.

Seek out all sources of information on programs that you might want to consider, and do your homework by carefully reviewing this material.

There are many other sources of relevant information to help you determine which program to apply to. Of course, if you select a field of study such as law or business or medicine, there are directories available that list all of the available programs. In some areas of graduate study directories and listings may be more difficult to find, and other sources of information may be needed. These directories should be available from professional societies, trade organizations, or even government agencies.

Directories that are properly prepared should include information about each program and possibly about the faculties. Some quantitative information may also be included, such as the admissions data mentioned above. Requirements for admission probably will also be listed. If there is an educational accrediting body in your field of study, the directory should indicate whether or not the school is accredited.

Accreditation is a measure of the program's having met certain national standards, although the importance of attending an accredited program depends on the field.

Accreditation is a process of certification whereby the program is reviewed by a panel of experts. A national accreditation body makes a determination of whether the program meets certain specified criteria and standards. Accreditation in some fields such as medicine is mandatory. In other fields, however, including law and many other graduate fields, accreditation is a little more elective. Generally, although not exclusively, the better programs will be accredited. But there are many decent programs that are not accredited for a variety of reasons. For example, new programs, regardless of quality, are frequently not accredited because many accreditation bodies require that a program graduate at least one class before any accreditation action is taken. Thus, while accreditation signals that a program meets minimum national standards, it is by no means the sole determination of quality.

Faculty members familiar with your intended field are excellent sources of information about programs worth considering.

Other indicators of the quality of a program relate more to a program's reputation, especially in the field of practice. The reputation of a program among faculty in other schools is a very important indicator of quality. You should ask local faculty who have a knowledge of the field that you wish to enter to list for you the best programs in the country. If you feel that your credentials are inadequate to obtain admission to the best programs, or if you have some other criteria such as geographic location, you might also ask about programs aside from these outstanding ones. Faculty in your intended field are among the best sources of information, since they usually know the reputation of the programs and other faculty around the country.

Practitioners can be an outstanding source of information, although they might not be up to date on all programs.

Another major source of information about the various programs is practitioners. Many practitioners are alumni of a program similar to the one you seek to enter and will have a very good perspective on the adequacy of many of the available programs. In addition, practitioners can also provide the perspective of a potential employer, which is after all the bottom line. Those programs that prepare students well for the "real world" of work will have a good reputation for finding graduates employment or postgraduate training positions.

Collect as much information as possible about the profession as well as the programs; talk to people, observe practitioners, and read any available information.

Talking to both academics and practitioners is invaluable. Not only can these people tell you about selected programs, they can also provide exceptional insights into the field you are seeking to enter. There is much to be said for entering a profession that will provide years of stimulation and satisfaction. Talking with people who work in the field every day can provide exposure to life-style, rewards, and headaches that you will eventually experience; the only other way to gain this experience is to work part-time or full-time in a related setting, such as in a law office, hospital, or research laboratory, where you can observe the activities of professionals. This is, of course, highly advisable as well.

The faculty of a program are more likely to feel assured about accepting students who know what they are getting into. Surprisingly, many people seek admission to fields of which they have little personal knowledge. This is sad because they really don't know what they are doing and, worse, may eventually drop out of school or be dissatisfied with their chosen career. It is shocking how little effort many people put into investigating the profession in which they will spend their entire working lives!

In selecting a school, think about your own needs and constraints.

In deciding which schools to apply to, you must also consider factors that are largely personal. For some people there

Choosing the School

are geographic limitations on where they can go for training. Since the number of reputable programs in any locality is usually limited, the applicant may be very restricted in training options.

Some individuals may be limited to certain schools because of financial constraints. More and more applicants are seeking advanced training in state-sponsored schools rather than in private universities, thus minimizing tuition expense. This obviously restricts the number of options. More financial aid may be available at some schools (as discussed in later chapters of this book), which may also bias applicants.

There are many other factors that can affect your selection of a school. Employed spouses will limit the available options. Sometimes people want to continue their training where they received their undergraduate degree. Thus, there are many personal considerations that legitimately should be included in your deliberations.

Whenever possible, the quality of available programs should be a major factor in determining where you apply.

The most important consideration should be the quality of the available programs. And if you want to specialize further while in training, you should explore the quality of the program in terms of your proposed area of specialization. For example, a medical school may have an outstanding national reputation but may be research oriented. If your interests are more in the area of family practice, you might be better off attending a program that has known strengths in that area. If you are interested in a business school but want to specialize in financial management, you should determine which schools are especially strong in that area. Given the degree of specialization in most professions these days, these more specific investigations can be of critical importance. On the other hand, many faculty would advise students not to become overspecialized, since this can lead to a loss of career flexibility. And the overall reputation of a university can often carry a graduate further than many would imagine.

Thus, the selection of programs is a rather complex task that requires that you thoroughly investigate the field of practice, the attributes of each program, and all personal factors that may enter into any decision. The more analytical applicant would be advised to write out, in a comparative tabular form, the attributes and deficiencies of each program.

Decide as early as possible to which programs you will apply—apply to as many as you feel will be needed to gain admission to at least one.

The decision about which programs to apply to may be relatively simple if, for example, there are significant geographic constraints and few acceptable programs. For many individuals, however, there will be quite a number of options. In some fields, such as medicine, there are some relatively common application procedures and even a national application process that must be followed. More often, however, each program has its own forms and procedures. Thus, it is important to obtain all available information for submitting application materials and to do so very early in the application process, allowing adequate time for the submission of required documentation. Schools that use a rolling admissions process, where each application is acted upon when complete, will inherently give preference to applicants whose files are completed earliest. Suggestions for contacting the school and for completing the forms are contained in the following chapters.

Inevitably, you will be faced with a decision about how many schools to apply to. There are no hard-and-fast rules to follow. All programs assume that they are competing with each other for the better candidates, and they all expect you to apply to more than one school. In fact, applicants who apply to only one school may be viewed a little suspiciously; if they really want to enter the profession, why are they limit-

Choosing the School

ing themselves so much at the front end? Are they more interested in the local entertainment available near the one school than in entering the field?

The average prospective medical student submits about eight applications. This number varies for other fields, but many people submit six or eight applications. How many you submit depends in part on where you are willing to go to school, the number of schools that you feel are worth applying to, and your endurance. In some specialized fields there may only be a few outstanding programs in the country that are worth considering.

Compile all of the available information, assess your personal preferences, and use your analytical skills and gut feelings to decide where to apply.

After you have assessed all of the available localities, personal preferences, and national reputations, you must make some judgments about which programs to apply to. Knowing how selective each program is and what your own qualifications are, and having discussed the available programs with practitioners and faculty, you can usually make a rational final decision. To be on the safe side you might include an extra program or two, especially ones that are relatively easy to get into. This gives you further options in the event that you are unsuccessful in gaining admission to your top choices.

There is probably a point of diminishing returns in applying to a very large number of programs.

It is unlikely that an applicant needs to apply to more than eight or ten programs. If that many applications are submitted and there are no acceptances, an even larger number probably won't lead to any acceptances either. Of course, while the marginal value of each added application after eight or ten decreases substantially, there is still a remote possibility of getting a letter of acceptance. It becomes, at the extreme, a question of endurance on the part of the applicant, to say nothing of the ability to pay application fees.

Choosing the school, then, involves a lot more than trying to guess which ones are likely to accept you. Your entire professional career may be determined by which school you attend. Careful thought must be directed toward the selection of programs; you will not regret the time so spent.

CHAPTER 4 *Initiating Contact with Your Future School*

EVERY CONTACT that an applicant has with a graduate or professional program before the admissions decision should be approached with caution. Even a request for information from a program should be handled with some degree of thoughtfulness. While it is unlikely that a messy letter requesting information is going to adversely affect your chances of admission, to be on the safe side every step in applying should be methodically handled. This includes even the initial contact with the school or program, since some programs retain in an applicant's file any early correspondence, even if it was only to request information.

Every contact with the program should be carefully conducted.

Once you have selected the programs to which you will apply, the mechanical processes begin in earnest. Your first step is to obtain information from each program in which you might be interested. This initial contact may occur prior to your final decision on which schools you will apply to, since the content of the curriculum and specific nature of the training program are usually discernible only from the brochures sent with the application packet.

The best way to initiate contact with your prospective program is by letter. You should request application forms for the term and specific program you prefer, along with all available information on the program. You should receive the materials within a month or so of this request, including information on the university and, sometimes, even on the city in which the university is located.

Some programs do not send a complete admissions packet to each initial inquiry. These programs may send a preliminary application or background information with a request that the applicant review the material and, if interested, then request more detailed information, including the complete application packet. The reason for this is fairly obvious. The costs of postage and of reproducing materials are increasing rapidly, and for a program that receives hundreds or thousands of inquiries these costs can be substantial. In addition, by sending only preliminary information, the program can prescreen potential applicants so that only those who are most interested will require follow-up.

Pay particular attention to all requirements and procedures for applying, to deadlines, special requests and standardized tests that are necessary.

In some instances, such as for medical schools, there are special application procedures that should be followed, starting with the first contact. It is usually important to follow the prescribed procedures, since they have been set up for specific reasons and probably work out relatively well. An admissions counselor at a local program or a faculty adviser may also be able to provide this type of information.

Initiating Contact with Your Future School

In your initial inquiry to the admissions office, provide some information about your specific training needs.

In your initial correspondence it may be advisable to provide a little information on your specific interests. If the program has a number of different areas of emphasis, this added information may help the admissions secretary provide you with more detailed information about those aspects of the curriculum that match your interests. In addition, if there is more than one training program in your general areas of interest at the university, your request for information can also be routed to these other programs. The amount of information that you provide need not be great, but it should be detailed enough so that the secretary can interpret what your educational interests are.

After you have received and carefully reviewed the materials from the program, you should fill out the application methodically, as discussed in the next chapter. But the completion of the application is only the beginning of a long process that culminates with the admissions decision.

Maintain contact with the program throughout the admissions process—always provide a current address and telephone number.

Many applicants fail to understand the importance of maintaining contact with the program even after they have completed the application. The processes of applying and of the subsequent reviews of candidates for admission often take six months or more. During this period it is imperative that you always keep in touch with the program. This contact takes a number of forms.

Of absolute importance is the need to keep the program informed of your current address and telephone number. The application is processed over a long period of time, during which you may change your residence or your telephone number. Since the program will need to keep in touch with you, it is essential that you keep this information current in the program's files. While this seems somewhat obvious, it is remarkable how many people fail to follow this simple rule. It can be very frustrating to the program secretary to try to contact an applicant only to find that mail is returned or the telephone has been disconnected.

In addition to a home telephone number, the wise applicant will also provide the program with a work telephone number and address, if any. However, if you prefer that your employer not know that you are seeking further education, you must tell the program to contact you discreetly.

Let the program know if you are having any difficulties in obtaining references, transcripts, or other important information.

You will also want to keep the program abreast of any significant difficulties you are having in providing the required information for completing your admissions file. Most programs will inform you of any deficiencies in your file such as missing letters of reference or grade transcripts. Ultimately, however, it is your responsibility to ensure that all of the necessary information is communicated to the program. This may at times be frustrating to you, but you are in fact best served by assuming the responsibility. Specifically, you should be sure that letters of reference are sent, that transcripts are ordered and will be sent, and that test scores are reported to the program. Since many programs use a rolling admissions procedure, where applications are acted upon as soon as the file is complete, it may be to your advantage to ensure that your application file is complete as soon as possible. On the other hand, it is also unwise to overly badger either the program or your sources of documentation. You should use common sense and be firm, but not offensive, in looking out for your best interests.

Consider taking advantage of any available counseling or guidance.

There are a number of other concerns that relate to the initiation and maintenance of contact with programs. Perhaps the most important of these is the availability of counseling. Many programs have either faculty or staff available to advise potential applicants. If you cannot determine the availability of such assistance from the application materials, feel free to ask the admissions secretary about it. If such counseling is available, it might be well worth taking advantage of it.

Counseling can be valuable to you. First, the admissions committee will know of your interest and, especially if you talk to a faculty member, will likely feel that you are a sincere applicant. However, you should always exercise the type of care and concern that would be recommended for a formal interview, as discussed in chapter 10.

Counseling also can provide you with insight into the admissions policies and procedures of the program. And finally, but certainly not least important, counseling can give you added valuable information about both the training program and the field of practice that you seek to enter. Most people can benefit from further information and guidance about their chosen field.

Some programs may also, in the process of accepting your application materials, offer to have you talk with alumni of the program or even some current students. Again, these opportunities are likely to be very worthwhile. Talking to current students about the program may be especially enlightening.

Take advantage of opportunities to maintain contact with the program—and add new positive information to your file when possible.

There still may be other opportunities to have contact with the program. Some people, for example, may have contact with faculty members through professional associations or meetings or other work-related interactions. As in all such situations, applicants should be on their best behavior, since they are likely to make some sort of impression on the faculty member that could conceivably be conveyed to the admissions committee. These less formal interactions are also an excellent and legitimate opportunity to ask intelligent questions concerning the program or even the field of practice.

Finally, you should feel free to contact the program throughout the admissions process. If there is new or additional information that can improve your application, ask that it be added to your file. This might include information on new jobs, awards, publications, and other achievements. Initiating and maintaining contact with the programs that you are interested in are not complex tasks, but it is necessary to be somewhat methodical and careful. Of course, the success-oriented applicant will want to follow such an approach at each step in applying for admission and in seeking financial aid.

PART II *Making Application*

CHAPTER 5 *Completing the Application Forms*

As everyone knows, first impressions are both important and long-lasting. So it should come as no surprise that the completion of the admissions forms themselves, which are the credentials usually first examined by the admissions committee, is worthy of your careful consideration. How completely and neatly the forms are filled out tells the admissions committee about your attitude toward the school and the professional program.

The application forms should be filled out carefully and completely.

The items of information requested on the application forms are required to present your credentials for review by the admissions committee. Surprisingly, however, many of the answers you provide may not be examined in detail or may be ignored by many of the individuals reviewing the file. Nevertheless, it is usually advisable to complete all of the items requested. Often the completeness with which you fill out the forms is taken as an indication of the extent to which you are serious about the program. The extent to which the application is completed may also be interpreted as a measure of your conscientiousness and ability to follow directions.

Complete all forms regardless of apparent duplication.

In graduate admissions it is not unusual for the applicant to be asked to complete more than one application form. While some of the information may be redundant, there is a logical explanation for the use of multiple application forms. Sometimes the candidate is required to complete separate program and university-wide or graduate admissions forms. The program forms are for use by the specific program or department to which you are applying and include detailed background information, questions concerning your career interests, and the like. These forms probably contain the most important information in terms of the admissions decision. Therefore, they require the utmost care in completing and will be most closely examined during the admissions process.

You may have to be admitted by both the program and the university or its graduate division—usually the latter is nearly automatic.

The university-wide forms, in contrast, usually contain relatively straightforward items which may even duplicate some of the application materials submitted directly to the program. These forms usually focus on general background information and the most basic academic information such as grades and test scores. They are far less likely to include subjective or qualitative information. These forms are usually required by the graduate division of the university or by a university-wide admissions office. Often an applicant is actually required to apply to, and be accepted by, both the graduate or professional program and the graduate school or the university admissions office.

Dual approval by the graduate division or university admissions office is usually a safeguard or double-check designed to ensure that the applicant meets the university's minimum requirements for graduate study. For the most part this assessment is based almost exclusively on the applicant's prior grade-point average and test scores on graduate or professional aptitude tests. Evaluation of credentials often involves automatic cutoffs. Students who fail to gain admission to the graduate division or university may still be conditionally admitted to the program.

Thus, the program admissions requirements are usually the more important of the two processes and evaluations. In addition, a student who fails to meet the graduate admissions requirements of the university often can be admitted on a probationary, or conditional, basis with such additional requirements as the achievement of a minimum grade-point average in the first semester. Finally, the criteria utilized by the graduate division or the university-wide admissions office are, for the most part, limited in scope. They usually examine the applicant based on standards which are frequently far lower than the criteria and standards of the program's own admissions committee.

This discussion suggests that where there are multiple admissions forms or procedures required, your greatest effort should be directed toward those required by the program itself. However, all forms must be carefully and completely filled out, since incomplete or poorly completed forms can significantly slow down the review of your credentials and even reduce your chances of admission.

To repeat, all application materials should be completed with the utmost care. Remarkably, many applicants appear to spend so little time on these forms that they hurt their chances of admission. Since these forms are carefully read by sensitive human beings, the attitude you reflect by your neatness and completeness is very important.

Application forms should be typed, when possible, and should always be neat, complete, legible, and accurate.

Application forms need not be typed. However, the appearance of the form is enhanced by typing, and therefore the extra effort to type the forms is quite justified. Marginal applicants may suggest a negative attitude to the program simply by the manner in which they complete the forms, regardless of the substance of their credentials. Surprisingly, some applicants submit forms that are mangled, illegible, incomplete, or incorrectly filled out. Remember that these forms are read by members of the admissions committee, who are judging your suitability for admission to the field of practice. How you present yourself may be interpreted as a reflection of your potential professionalism. Although an outstanding applicant can probably get away with a lot, even applicants with very good academic credentials are sometimes rejected. The wise applicant will leave nothing to chance.

Answer questions openly and completely, but present information in a favorable light.

All of the questions asked on the form should be answered, generally speaking, in a forthright and open manner. Any appearance that you are hiding information, even inadvertently, should be avoided. Most questions on the application forms, with the exception of any essay questions or narratives, should be relatively easy to answer. Some of the questions may appear poorly written or irrelevant. Indeed, many application forms are not very well designed. However, it is not your place as an applicant to point this out.

Most questions relate to your demographic characteristics, the history of schools attended, jobs held, and the like. While there is some potential for discrimination based on your responses to these types of questions, you should provide all of

Completing the Application Forms

the information that is requested anyway. Discrimination based on sex or age is difficult to control and is controversial in those schools where it is practiced, such as in medical schools. Anyway, most of the information is apparent from your transcripts or other available information, and failure to complete items may raise red flags for no good purpose.

Optional or elective questions probably should be answered only if they help your cause.

The completion of some items may be elective or voluntary. These should be carefully considered by the applicant. Requests for religious preference in a church-affiliated school may help or hinder—this is difficult to judge except in individual circumstances. For all optional questions you need to consider the reasons the information is being requested and what the likely effect of answering or not answering may be.

Racial minorities should let this affiliation be known— other minorities should be more discreet.

An elective question on your race should be completed by minority applicants. Programs need to know if they are attracting applications from minorities, and this information is often used to further such efforts. There may be preference given for admission of minority applicants, and any discrimination in graduate and professional programs, while it certainly still may exist in some instances, is probably now far outweighed by the extra consideration given minorities. Since the objective of this book is to give all applicants advice on improving their chances of admission, minority applicants have to be advised to use every available opportunity. And if this information is not directly asked, racial minorities should ensure that it is provided through such information as affiliation with minority organizations, volunteer work, and the like. Women and other minorities who may very well be discriminated against should seriously consider providing as little information as possible relating to their minority status. This advice probably also applies to political affiliations and preferences and personal attitudes toward controversial social issues.

Other interesting questions that may be asked in the application forms include whether any of your relatives are graduates of the university to which you are now applying. A positive response can do little harm, and it may help, especially if you are highly qualified and competing for one of a limited number of available positions. You may also be asked where you heard about the program. This should be answered honestly and is not usually an important question. If you list a member of the faculty or an alumnus of the program, you will reflect previous investigation and knowledge of the program.

List all schools attended, especially any where you completed graduate courses and did well.

Usually you will be asked to list all schools attended past secondary school, and there is no reason not to do so. However, if you only took one or two courses and they were not related to a degree program, you may not want to list them if you did poorly. The main objective of this question is to elicit all of the schools in which you were a degree candidate, regardless of whether you completed the program. Your answer will be compared to the transcripts in your file, so be sure that all of the schools you have attended send transcripts to the program. If you attended a school but then transferred to another to complete your degree, you should list both schools.

If you attended a school for only one or two courses, but they were graduate-level courses and you did well, be sure to list them and arrange for transcripts, since they help demonstrate your ability to do graduate-level work. If you attended a school or program in the same field for which you are now applying, you will have to explain your reasons for dropping out and then seeking to reenter the field.

Work experience is important, especially if it is in the field you want to enter.

Most likely you will also be asked to list all your work experience. There may be separate questions on paid and voluntary work, full-time and part-time work. You may also have to separate experience that is directly related to your chosen field from other work experience. Your work experience may be examined in considerable detail, especially in areas related to the field you are seeking to enter. In addition, work experience reflects your commitment to the field of practice. Prior practical exposure to the field helps assure the admissions committee that you know what you are getting into, and therefore it is usually a positive factor, as discussed in detail in chapter 9.

Full-time work experience generally counts more than part-time or volunteer work, but all relevant experience should be reported.

Full-time work experience generally counts more than part-time experience, and paid employment usually counts more than equivalent volunteer work. In fields such as medicine or dentistry there may be less concern over whether or not you were paid and more concern that you have been exposed to the front lines of the field; for example, you may have done volunteer work in a hospital emergency room as a patient's aide. Since there is little you can do to change your employment history, your primary concerns should be to present an honest picture and to impress the admissions committee with any meaningful service that you have performed.

Keep in mind that most members of the admissions committee have seen just about every possible approach by applicants who overrepresent their experience. It is unlikely that you can successfully make your experience appear to be much more than it really is. In addition, you always run the risk that someone will check up on your experience with a phone call. Therefore, there is little value in exaggeration, although there is nothing wrong in making the most out of your experience.

Make the most of your experience and point out any supervisory or unusual duties that may reflect motivation, skills, enthusiasm, success potential, or other positive attributes.

If you have the opportunity to elaborate in detail on your experience, it is almost always beneficial to do so; be sure to point out any instances in which your actual duties and responsibilities exceeded what your title would indicate. For example, you may have been asked to assume administrative or supervisory duty or to undertake a special project, even though such activities were outside the normal scope of your job. In such instances the admissions committee may be impressed by your added responsibilities and initiative or by the confidence that your supervisor appeared to have in your abilities. Pointing out these types of experiences can show that your employment was more important than it might appear to be on paper from job titles. You may also want to point out this type of information in interviews or in your narrative statement.

If your job titles do not accurately reflect your actual responsibilities, you might consider listing in parentheses, next to your official title, some phrase that is more descriptive and more impressive. Remember that you are not strictly limited to providing the exact information that is requested. You can always elaborate on information as long as it is supportive to your application and there is space available on the forms. You can also usually add more sheets of paper on which additional information can be provided. The application is thus an opportunity to present information that you want the admissions committee to review, in addition to what they want submitted.

Provide any quantitative information as accurately as possible.

You may also be asked to provide academic information. Most commonly applicants are asked to estimate their undergraduate or graduate grade-point average, to list standardized test scores, and to list courses completed. This information is often redundant since it is usually available to the committee from other sources, but it is usually requested for the convenience of the admissions office. These factual items should be accurately provided as requested. Since the committee has the information anyway, exaggeration of your grades or test scores will appear highly deceptive. However, for grades, your estimates may be rounded upward. For example, a 3.46 could be listed as a 3.5 as long as you are not required to give your grade-point average to two decimal places. Again, you will want any impressions that you leave on whoever reads your file to be as positive as possible.

The application may also require that you provide references. This list is used in most instances to keep track of when your letters of reference are received, and so it should be accurate. In addition, you should report to the program any change in references. List these people so that they appear as impressive as possible, perhaps including degrees, titles, and full names. This is also another opportunity to impress the committee with the care you have taken in completing your application.

The application form is an extremely important opportunity to provide additional impressive information, regardless of whether it is requested by the admissions committee.

As noted previously, the application is a valuable opportunity to provide additional supportive information to the admissions committee. You are rarely forbidden to include additional sheets of information with your application, especially if they can somehow be related to the questions asked in the printed forms. For example, the information requested on your previous employment provides an opportunity to include a detailed list of employment experiences. This list can include an impressive presentation of the unique duties and responsibilities of your various jobs. You can point out unusual responsibilities that you assumed and anything else that reflects positively on your intellectual abilities, creativity, professionalism, and innovation. You can present yourself as a thinker and doer. Again, overelaboration or misrepresentation should be avoided. In addition, exceptional achievements, such as important scientific advances or a rapid rise in the corporate hierarchy, should be supported by a letter of reference from a supervisor.

There are, of course, other areas in which supplementary information may be useful. These will become more apparent as you thoughtfully review your strengths and weaknesses. Weaknesses need not be elaborated, but all relevant strengths should be emphasized if there is an opportunity to do so. This may be accomplished through the personal interview, through presentation of academic credentials, through the skillful preparation of a narrative statement, or, as discussed above, through the inclusion of supplemental material in the application.

Many topics can be covered in person, but programs often do not require interviews. In addition, information conveyed in the interview may never be communicated to the admissions committee. Therefore, the written application may be the best way to provide supplemental information and explanations that you want to have considered on your behalf.

Use the application form to explain potential problem areas in your credentials and background, but be careful not to raise any red flags or to emphasize prior difficulties.

Supplemental application information can be used to describe unusual or extenuating circumstances explaining any problems in your record that might be of concern to the admissions committee. For example, explanations of periods of illness or personal or family problems that led to some poor grades can help to offset the effect of those grades, especially if there is other evidence of academic ability. Such explanations should be kept short and to the point; otherwise they are unlikely to be completely and carefully read, and may overemphasize the problem. Be careful not to create problems that don't actually exist.

In some instances it may be useful to include a curriculum vitae or résumé in your application. This can be valuable if you have a considerable amount of work experience or other elaborate credentials that must be communicated to the admissions committee. However, if the information is already available on the application, a résumé should not be included.

A narrative or personal statement, if required, is of extreme importance and gives you an opportunity to plead your case to the admissions committee.

There is also another very important opportunity for providing additional information. Many programs require that the applicant submit a personal statement or narrative. This can be an exceedingly important document and must be carefully written and rewritten in the best possible style.

The narrative statement will be used by the program not

only to determine your career interests, professional objectives, and commitment to the field of practice, but also to get a broad view of your credentials. It is also used as a reflection of your ability, intellectual strengths, and your ability to think logically. A poor narrative can be devastating, yet many applicants pay far too little attention to its preparation.

The narrative should, first, address any specific questions that are asked on the application form. Second, the narrative should be used as an opportunity for you to make your pitch about why you are so good and should be admitted both to the program and to the field of practice. You may want to explain how this particular program will exactly meet your needs and to detail your obviously well-thought-out career interests. Do not be so specific in your interests that the admissions committee may feel the program will not meet your training needs. Also remember that most people frequently change their specific interests over time and that your narrative is not a long-term commitment. Rather, it is a statement of intent that should make the admissions committee feel good about accepting you.

The narrative statement should be concise, well written, and to the point—avoid irrelevant and unnecessary verbiage.

Narrative statements should avoid long theoretical discussions and philosophical essays—unless specifically requested. They should be extremely well written and have no errors in spelling or grammar. The wise applicant will go through more than one draft and perhaps even show the narrative to a friend, preferably an English major, for an outside opinion. You should emphasize your specific interests and your potential for contributing to the field. The narrative is also an opportunity to explain any unusual situations, and to elaborate on your skills, aptitudes, interests, and knowledge.

You may want to impress the admission committee by noting unusual talent and achievements in competitive sports, music, or the performing arts. Indeed, many programs seek out well-rounded individuals, and outstanding accomplishments in a number of arenas can be most impressive. In addition, talents in the arts, in languages, or in other fields often give an impression of high intellectual abilities.

Thus, the narrative statement deserves the utmost care in completion and should be one of your major selling opportunities. It should also be positive, forthright, and grammatically impeccable.

Essay questions, as with the personal statement, should be clearly and concisely answered; responses must be well written, thoughtful, and analytical.

You may also be asked to answer a series of essay questions. These may be specific or general questions designed to determine your knowledge of the field of practice, your substantive knowledge of topics covered in college courses, or the relevance of your past experiences and interests. The range of questions can be quite broad. You may be asked to discuss your personal philosophy, to list the books you have recently read, or to give your opinions about the field you seek to enter and how you would function as a professional.

Essay questions may be carefully and critically reviewed by the admissions committee. They must be answered with the same care and thoughtfulness that should be expended on the narrative statement. Inflammatory or highly emotional comments should generally be avoided. All questions should be directly and openly answered. Statements that reflect a specific attitude or philosophy, if they sound analytical and logical, should not harm your chances. You need not be a Casper Milquetoast, but your answers should reflect the fact that you are a mature, thoughtful individual. If you are asked specific questions, you should provide specific answers. Do not ramble or present irrelevant topics. Your responses should sound professional and reasonably intellectual without being stuffy. Above all, take the time to write and rewrite enough to ensure well-prepared, impressive responses.

There is an almost bizarre range of other types of questions that you may be asked in the application forms. Most are of an informational nature, and all should be answered carefully. Think about why the school might be asking each question before formulating your answers. While your answers should always be truthful, you should also use the "best-sounding" answer or phrases. Always read and rewrite your responses before completing the original application forms. You may want to use a reproduced copy of the forms to draft your answers. Then read them from the perspective of the admissions committee. How does each answer strike you? Could the edge be taken off any responses? Are any answers unduly vague? Do any answers give the appearance of being deceptive?

When you have answered all questions in a professional way, see to it that the final version is typed or, if necessary, neatly printed. Proofread everything carefully. To complete the professional appearance, the envelope should be typed and include a return address. A brief cover letter may be prepared and included for formality, then the entire package should be neatly sealed for mailing. One can only hope that the postal service provides as much care for your materials as you have. For further insurance, certified postage, with an acknowledgment of receipt requested, may be wise. Always keep a copy of all material for your files.

Certainly the application forms themselves are not as important in any admissions decision as your grades and test scores. On the other hand, poorly prepared essays and narratives can have an adverse effect. In the final analysis the extra care required for an obviously professionally prepared application is a small price to pay for the added insurance that your application will receive serious consideration. And how seriously you take the application may provide a hint to the admissions committee on how serious you intend to be about graduate or professional school.

CHAPTER 6 *References and Other Testimonials to Your Potential*

THE SELECTION OF REFERENCES is a rather traumatic experience. Many applicants, for fear of selecting someone who might harbor a hidden grudge, fail to easily identify people who can act as references. There should be little reason for concern, however.

References are less important than you may think.

References, ideally, provide outside, objective opinions of candidates whom they have known professionally or personally. Unfortunately, the ways references are selected, and the recommendation forms completed, are often very imperfect. Most candidates select as references people who are likely to give them a favorable review. And these people often are hesitant to write a negative report, knowing that such a recommendation, in this era of largely positive reviews, could mean failure for an applicant. As a result, the recommendation process has become somewhat watered down, and usually is less significant than many applicants realize.

Strong references can help strengthen an application.

Of course, it is still very important to select references carefully. These days references that sound negative or that raise serious questions about the applicant's capabilities can be very damaging. The references should at least be neutral. And unusually positive references from very reputable people can have a positive effect. But rarely can references carry enough weight to overcome poor grades or test scores; they can only partially offset a lack of experience or similar factors.

References should be written and formal.

Most schools require two or three letters of reference, occasionally more and rarely less. References should be conveyed in writing. Even if your references are personally known to members of the admissions committee, they should convey comments in writing and not by telephone. And these written comments should always be in a formal letter or on the school's forms. In this way all members of the admissions committee will be able to review the written comments of your reference. The physical appearance of a letter testifying to your skills and abilities is more impressive than an informal note or phone call.

The applicant has little control over the form or substance of letters of reference. Most people who are asked to write letters of reference, especially faculty members, will not only be aware of the desired format but will also know the importance of positive content.

Select as references people who can write strong, positive letters.

Since you will submit only a few letters of reference, the selection of individuals to argue on your behalf is very important. It is not necessary to ask more people to write letters of reference for you than the school requires, but your initial selection of references must be carefully thought out.

References should reflect an applicant's academic or professional ability.

Most graduate and professional schools want letters of reference to add to their knowledge of the applicant in two areas: academic ability and professional potential. By and large, the main emphasis on letters of reference is in the former area. Especially in graduate programs, the letters of reference are important in assuring the school of the candidate's true academic and intellectual abilities. In professional programs these are also important concerns, but there is often further consideration given to the candidate's potential as a professional in the field of practice.

Some programs will specify in detail how many of each type of reference must be submitted; for example, such and such a number from past teachers, such and such from prior work colleagues or supervisors. In those programs that specify the total number of required references, the applicant must use careful judgment in deciding whom to ask for a letter of reference.

References are worth time and thought.

Many applicants consider letters of reference merely pro forma exercises and ask the first people whose names come to mind. As with other aspects of the admissions process discussed in this book, a more analytical approach is recommended. Some careful thinking may lead to references that have more impact. This chapter provides guidelines to achieve this.

Letters related to academic ability should emphasize an applicant's strengths and explain or justify weaknesses.

The most important letters of reference are usually those that relate to the applicant's academic potential. For the fortunate applicants with extremely strong grades and test scores there is little need for the additional evidence of academic ability, and some letters of reference might be directed toward other areas of potential concern, such as maturity and motivation. For applicants with less than optimal grades, letters of reference addressing their abilities and explaining the lower-than-desirable performance may be very important.

Thus, the bottom line for letters of reference is to ensure adequate reinforcement of your academic credentials while at the same time addressing any of your potential areas of weakness. Exactly where these areas of weakness are should be assessed by the applicant. This is usually somewhat easy to do, especially with the help of counseling from a friendly faculty member or practicing professional. Indeed, all applicants should honestly and critically assess their individual strengths and weaknesses.

The best letters of reference related to scholastic ability are from faculty members.

In the area of academic ability there is virtually no alternative to letters of reference from faculty members in the college or graduate programs that an applicant has attended. Most admissions committee members are academics, who attribute considerable credence to other academics when assessing students' intellectual abilities. No number of letters from friends or professional colleagues can match the value of a strong letter of reference from a solid member of a respected university faculty in terms of assessing and supporting a student's academic ability. An unusually supportive letter from a senior faculty member may actually partially offset some of the effects of less-than-optimal grades or test scores.

Academic letters of reference should be from former teachers when possible.

Letters of support from academic faculty should be, first and foremost, from faculty members who know the applicant as a student, not just as a friend. A very businesslike letter that ascribes great wonders to the student's ability in the classroom is much more useful than a friendly letter from a faculty member who raves about how nice a person the student is. The combination of both perspectives, of course, is most desirable.

Most students have considerable apprehension about which faculty members to ask for a letter of reference. In many schools—especially at the undergraduate level, where classes are large and there are many majors in an undergraduate field—most students have relatively little contact with faculty members. The wise student will attempt, especially during the junior and senior years, to be known by and to impress at least a few faculty members. In many instances the student will have a faculty adviser who is aware, to some extent, of the student's progress and abilities. Unfortunately, the adviser may not have taught the student and therefore may not be as effective a reference as a classroom teacher would be.

In addition to classroom teachers, other faculty may be useful as references. If a student worked part-time for a faculty member, especially as a teaching assistant or as a research assistant on a serious project, he or she might have an ideal opportunity to have someone testify to their outstanding potential for professional development. Independent or special studies, when they are rigorous and serious, can lead to a relatively close relationship between student and teacher and another chance for a letter of reference. And any other formal contact with faculty members that has an academic content may have the potential for a letter of reference.

Thus, at least one letter of reference, and sometimes more, should be from classroom teachers. Perhaps one more could be from a faculty member with whom the student worked or had other formal academic contact. And a third letter could be from a professional associate or employer or from another faculty member. Each letter of reference should be a positive addition to the applicant's credentials.

The best references are from teachers in hard academic courses related to the field one seeks to enter.

The letters of reference from academic faculty should be from those people who are in either the student's chosen graduate or professional field or in a related area. Letters of reference in so-called soft fields or in nonrigorous areas should be avoided. For example, an applicant to a program in art history should have letters of reference from undergraduate instructors in the area of art, preferably in topics specifically related to art history. These letters should reflect the student's success thus far in the field and the tremendous aptitude and potential that the student has in the area of art history. An applicant to a science program, on the other hand, would benefit very little, if at all, from a letter from an art teacher; these students should have letters of reference from teachers in science courses.

Faculty with whom you completed several courses are generally better sources of reference than those from whom you had only one course, especially if you completed a sequence of related courses, doubly so if these were academically rigorous courses. In other words, the more exposure that the faculty member had to you, assuming that it was a positive exposure, the better a letter of reference he or she can write, and the more impressive the reference will appear to the admissions committee.

Selecting as references faculty who taught you in especially easy courses, or in the few courses for which you have good grades, will probably have little positive effect. Most admissions committee members are very aware of which courses are easy, and they also have a copy of your transcript. Letters of reference from faculty from whom you got respectable, but not outstanding grades, and which point out any extenuating circumstances and attest to your innate abilities, can be much more effective. If you have only a few courses with good grades, you might not be an appropriate candidate for advanced study.

A *reference can explain deficiencies in the applicant's credentials.*

A reference can be an effective means of explaining a legitimate but not fatal weakness in your credentials. Indeed, a faculty member or other reference can be much more influential in these instances than can the applicant. Extenuating circumstances may include personal problems that are likely to have been resolved by the time of matriculation into graduate or professional school, illnesses that affected academic performance, or other situations that affected undergraduate performance but are unlikely to affect future school work. Some very effective letters of reference have been written detailing how individuals raised themselves out of poor beginnings and overcame socioeconomically or academically disadvantaged backgrounds. The academic rigor of the program you seek to enter will largely determine how accepting of such situations the admissions committee will be.

When these unusual situations exist, the applicant should not hesitate to ask the person writing the letter of reference to address them. In many instances you can directly ask a reference to address specific issues in his or her letter. Most applicants fail to realize how willing reference writers often are to do this. The strategy can substantially strengthen your application and can make an important difference if the area of concern was troubling the admissions committee. Obviously, if the reference addresses the concern in a negative context, serious damage can result. Thus, some caution is essential, and the applicant might consider going so far as to ask the references what they would say about the issue.

Professional programs are often concerned with more than just the academic potential of the student and may require references from people other than faculty members. Graduate programs tend to be less interested in nonacademic references. The applicant should be guided by the instructions provided by the program. If there is inadequate information on the subject in the application materials, you may even want to call and ask specifically what the desired mix of references is.

Professional references must be carefully selected to ensure credibility.

The applicant should carefully consider the objectives of references from sources other than academic faculty. Many applicants waste important opportunities by the selection of references who contribute little if anything to their credentials. This is most true of nonacademic references.

In most instances, and especially in professional programs, the objective of seeking at least some references from nonacademics is to determine the applicant's potential for personal and professional development. In particular, such references can attest to the high moral standing of the applicant and to the tremendous potential of the individual as a contributing professional in the field of practice. Recall that the admissions committee is admitting the student to the profession in addition to admitting him or her to the program. Therefore, the committtee wants to be assured that the individual will be a credit to both program and profession. This is one area in which one or two nonacademic references can be very supportive.

Professional references should generally be from people who have been exposed to the student in a professional situation; this is especially important for applicants to professional schools. The most useful references for the applicant, and for the admissions committee, are from individuals who have supervised or worked with the applicant in a professional setting, preferably one related to the type of program for which the application is being submitted. Ideally, this type of letter of reference is from an established practitioner in the field and discusses the applicant's maturity, competence, and tremendous potential for contributing to the profession.

Professional references should reflect the applicant's maturity, commitment, and potential as a professional.

This type of letter could result from full-time paid employment, part-time employment, or even volunteer work. The important points of such letters are that they come from established professionals and that they attest to the applicant's potential for professional success. A very strong letter along these lines might help balance some questionable aspects of the applicant's academic credentials, but, as always, there is a limit to which anything can overcome the effects of poor grades or low test scores.

Professional references should be from supervisors who knew you well.

Letters of reference from friends or associates at work are much less impressive than those from supervisors or from higher-level management. The more established the writer of the letter of reference is in the field of practice, the better. However, letters of reference from people who had little direct contact with you are not nearly as meaningful as those from individuals with extensive exposure over a period of time.

Requesting letters of reference from friends, from clergy, and from family members is generally not worthwhile. These letters are usually ignored. They may be necessary if the school specifically requests them, such as a letter from a clergyman for an applicant to a religious school, but this is a special case. Letters from family friends who talk about how they watched you grow up and how wonderful you are have little worth and may be taken as evidence of your inability to obtain solid letters from more meaningful or relevant sources.

Many applicants wonder about the value of letters of reference from influential persons. This is a touchy topic for obvious reasons, and any efforts to exert pressure on a program to admit someone can readily backfire; on the other hand, such efforts can also succeed at times. The best advice may be to avoid pressuring the program if there is adequate support in your credentials to ensure a good probability of admission, as discussed in chapter 11.

Letters of support from well-known and influential people usually are not very impressive to the admissions committee when they are quickly drafted, reflect little personal knowledge of the applicant, or appear to be a form letter without much true substance. In those instances where an applicant may actually have worked for such an individual, of course, the letter of reference may be quite useful. For the most part, however, admissions committees know that many well-known people write laudatory letters of vague support for people they don't really know.

Provide your references with the necessary forms and information for responding.

The letter of reference, as noted previously, usually should be prepared on the official school forms provided by the program. People submitting a letter on behalf of an applicant may prefer to write on their own stationery rather than the official form, and this should be of little concern to the applicant. What is more important is that the applicant provide the reference with any official forms or instructions from the program concerning the desired content and format, along with a preaddressed, stamped envelope for use in sending the forms back to the program. A little courtesy goes a long way—this is an appropriate time to make another positive impression.

Applicants may also provide the reference with a written or oral statement about their career goals, why this particular school was selected, and why this individual was asked to write a letter of reference. Do not be bashful; such information can help the person writing the letter of reference provide further evidence that you know what you are doing in terms of career goals and program selection. While you do not want to badger the reference, most people will very much appreciate this type of information and will use it in composing their letters. In addition, this is an opportunity to ask that any special circumstances in your background be addressed by a relatively objective reviewer. You might also note the importance of returning the letter to the program as soon as possible.

Although committee or on-file letters are acceptable, specially written, personal letters are usually more impressive.

In some undergraduate institutions letters of reference are routinely collected and maintained in a central file for future use by the student. These are usually letters from faculty members and definitely should be used. They are simple to request and will serve as useful letters of support, if they are positive. Often the student will have seen these letters in advance so that their content is no surprise. However, these are not as helpful as individual letters that address an applicant's specific selection of a program of study, and they are usually rather abbreviated and limited in scope. Therefore, even with the availability of these on-file letters of reference, the applicant should consider requesting additional personal letters from other faculty and from practitioners, where appropriate. These additional letters can address the issues that are unique to the student's individual situation and can supplement the more routine content of the on-file letters.

Perhaps most frustrating of all forms of letters are committee letters because they are not very personal and reflect consensus opinion. These composite letters, routinely drawn up in many universities, are frequently prepared and signed on behalf of a preprofessional committee. They are based on accumulated comments contained in the student's preprofessional file and summarize the views of all relevant instructors and advisers. As such, they may be unusually critical of the applicant, and may be more accurate than the usual letter of reference or than the applicant might want. In such cases, it might be a good idea to request personal letters from individual instructors, or from other references.

You may be requested to waive your right to review letters of reference; there is no reason not to sign.

In submitting the letter-of-reference forms, you may be requested to sign a statement waiving your right to read the letters at a future time. Because of legal developments in the area of student rights over the past twenty years, in most institutions students have a right to examine their academic file. Signing the statement usually waives this right with respect to the letters of reference. The assumption is that the letter writer will be more frank knowing that you will never see the letter. While it is up to the applicant to decide whether or not to sign, there is little reason not to do so. Actually, the content of the letter probably will not be very different either way. Indeed, many people who write letters of reference are happy to provide the applicant with a copy if so requested.

Avoid obtaining negative letters of reference.

Most letters of reference are favorable, and candidates are often unduly apprehensive about them. While a negative letter does stand out and may be a significant adverse factor, many potential writers will warn an applicant directly or indirectly that they do not feel comfortable writing a positive or enthusiastic letter. In these cases don't push the point; rather, thank the individual for their consideration of your request and seek letters elsewhere.

It might even be wise to ask prospective references if they would be comfortable writing a supportive letter for you. There is no reason why you cannot ask such a question, and many people would rather tell you to seek a letter elsewhere, which they can do in a polite and nonthreatening way, than damage your chances of admission. But, again, since a negative letter can have severe consequences regardless of who it is from, think through who would be your best references and approach them openly, providing information that they can use to strengthen your application.

There are some other special circumstances that are worthy of note. If you have previously completed part or all of a graduate program, you should have one or more of your letters of reference from faculty members in that program. They can attest to your ability to handle graduate-level work and can explain any unusual circumstances that may have led to your failure to complete the program, if that was the case. In addition, they might address why you are now applying for another graduate program in the same or a different field of study. Demonstration of your ability to perform graduate work is perhaps the most important aspect of applying for advanced study; it should be emphasized at any possible point in the admissions process.

Letters of reference should be current, positive, and well written.

Letters of reference that were written long ago and are not up-to-date are nice for historical purposes but really say little about your current career interests, abilities, and personality. Therefore, most letters of reference should be relatively current. But a letter or two from an undergraduate teacher can be useful even though it is old information about the level of intellectual ability and the outstanding personality you once had. This is especially important for someone who has been working for a number of years and has not taken courses recently.

In summary, the letters of reference are another opportunity for you to strengthen your application. They should be carefully assessed, and the individuals who write them should be able to make strong positive statements about your academic ability, potential professional development, and mature personality. Although many admissions committees look more for letters of reference from former teachers, the applicant's potential as a professional may also be addressed through letters of reference from nonacademics.

In the final analysis, letters of reference should at the very least do no harm. And for most applicants this is about all they do. But the wise applicant will also recognize the potential for letters of reference to do some good.

CHAPTER 7 *Quantitative Data on Your Past: Prior Training and Grades*

THERE ARE TWO TYPES of quantitative data on which the admissions decision is at least partially based. These are your prior academic achievements as reflected by grades, schools and programs attended, and courses of study, and then your standardized test scores. Your academic record is the subject of this chapter, while the test scores are addressed in the following chapter.

Your academic record is essentially cast in concrete by the time you apply to graduate or professional school.

There is relatively little that you can do to change the quantitative record from your prior training. Wise students will consider the likelihood of seeking admission to graduate school as one factor in deciding how hard they work in college. The sad truth is that the records of many potential candidates are not overly impressive.

Grades are usually the single most important factor in admissions.

Nevertheless, grades are only one factor in the evaluation of a student's academic credentials. They do not stand alone;

rather, they are almost always considered in conjunction with other attributes.

The better the college you attended, the more rigorous its program, and the better your performance, the greater is your admissions advantage.

The United States is fortunate to have a large, diverse, and for the most part high-quality educational "system," but college-level programs differ substantially when the education they offer is measured in terms of rigor, academic quality, difficulty in achieving high grades, and other similarly imprecise indicators of how "good" a school or program is. It is only natural that the admissions committee seeks assurance that you attended a high-quality college and pursued a program that prepared you well to continue your education. Many programs also pride themselves on their ability to recruit top students from the best undergraduate institutions.

Evaluating schools and programs is not easy, nor is the process necessarily as objective as many people would like to believe. The assessment of universities and colleges is based for the most part on subjective evidence and vague indicators of reputation, frequently without recognizing the individual student's actual program of study or departmental affiliation. The assessment of a program, when it occurs in any detail, is usually based on the reputation of the program's graduates and faculty and on its overall national recognition.

The assessments of your college will likely be based on such vague measures as its national reputation and visibility, sometimes without consideration of your actual program or department.

There are sharp differences in the extent to which various colleges and universities are nationally recognized for the quality of the education that they provide. Some have instant recognition anywhere in the world, while others are only known in their communities. The lack of a national or international reputation may be an adverse factor, even if the college has a fine local reputation. The admissions committee may be totally unaware of this local reputation, especially when your school is distantly located. This is unfortunate, because many less well-known institutions are quite good when it comes to undergraduate education, sometimes surpassing much better-known institutions.

Almost everyone has heard of the nation's top colleges and universities, and there is little likelihood that the members of the admissions committee will not also have heard of them. If you have attended Harvard or Michigan or some such school, you will have name recognition on your side. However, many applicants have not attended the nation's best-known schools. For them the evaluation of their institutions of higher learning becomes more difficult for the admissions committee.

You may be better off if someone from your university has previously attended the program you are applying to and has done well. Many less well-known colleges consistently send top-notch students to certain prestigious graduate or professional schools, and as long as these students do well the gates may remain open for more graduates.

In this regard, it might be a good idea to talk to your professors. They will be a good source of knowledge about which of their students have gone where, and how they are doing. Remember that admissions committees prefer known quantities and like to accept students from colleges with good track records. You might even want to consider transferring to another college where your chances of admission will be enhanced by such a track record.

The more "selective" your college, as measured by difficulty of undergraduate admissions, the more impressed the admissions committee is likely to be.

The assessment of schools is often based on general reputation, which means what people on the admissions committee generally think of the school. When more quantitative information is required, the committee will often use scales of admissions selectivity at the undergraduate level. These scales are crude and somewhat subjective. They usually include such categories as "very selective," "selective," and so forth. Various publications that list American colleges and universities include these scales. The admissions committee or staff may assign a number to the selectivity scale for use in assessing the "quality" of your prior education.

The moral of the story is that there may be some bias in favor of applicants who attended and did well at the best schools, as measured by national reputation or selectivity. While the educational program may not be any better at these schools than at less well-known institutions, the overall reputation can still be very influential. Of course, since there are many factors included in the admissions decision, the choice of what college to attend should never be based solely on your long-term education goals. But, all things considered, the choice of a university or college with an outstanding overall national reputation could be a plus for the student who eventually will seek further degrees.

Some undergraduate programs are well known and carry with them considerable prestige for graduates.

Rather than attempt to assess in detail the quality of the educational institution you attended for college, some admissions committees will focus on the specific program you were enrolled in. Many undergraduate programs do have national or, at the least, regional reputations. Sometimes an undergraduate program has the advantage of being sponsored by the same department that offers a very prestigious graduate program, or the undergraduate program itself may even be well known because of its excellence or the accomplishments of its graduates.

If the admissions committee members are personally familiar with the undergraduate program you attended, and if that program has a good reputation, you are in a relatively favorable position—assuming that your performance was also respectable. If you earned an undergraduate degree in the same field as your proposed graduate program, and if you did well, you may be in a particularly advantageous situation: You will have demonstrated competence in your field and will have completed many preliminary courses for advanced study. However, there are some fields in which it is not desirable to have an undergraduate degree in the same area as your proposed graduate progam. This is especially true in professional fields for which the undergraduate degree is viewed as a poor imitation of graduate training and as inappropriate preparation.

Your undergraduate major is important in terms of rigor and academic difficulty, value as preparation for advanced study, and overall relevance.

Most admissions committees will examine your undergraduate field of study from a couple of perspectives. First, the committee is interested in the appropriateness of the field to your proposed plan for graduate or professional training. While there is not usually a narrowly defined set of acceptable undergraduate majors, there are also some fields which simply do not mesh. And there are majors at the undergraduate level that naturally precede certain fields of graduate study.

The degree to which any specific undergraduate major field of study meets the needs of someone entering graduate study can vary considerably. There are few rules in this area. Many programs will provide some information, either routinely or on request, concerning the best undergraduate preparation, if any. But for many applicants it is too late to heed this advice by the time they are applying to graduate or professional school. In some instances, such as medicine or dentistry, there are prerequisite courses that must be completed, regardless of your major.

A second concern of the admissions committee with regard to the undergraduate major is the degree of difficulty of the field of study and of the specific courses that you completed. A "soft," or easy, major clearly raises a red flag, except if you seek further education in the same field.

Good grades in a hard major and in difficult, academically rigorous courses are the best demonstration of ability in the classroom.

Good grades in a weak field of study may be less impressive than poor grades in a harder field. Unfortunately, it is not possible to suggest the optimal combination of courses and majors that are hard enough to look good but easy enough to ensure good grades.

A major field of study that is very weak in academic rigor can also be partially counterbalanced by the completion of a number of courses, perhaps five or six, that are clearly rigorous and difficult. These additional courses might even be at the graduate level.

There are no hard-and-fast rules about which majors and courses any particular admissions committee will consider hard or soft. In general, but not universally, the so-called hard sciences, including engineering, would be considered the most difficult areas of study, followed by rigorous disciplines in the soft sciences such as economics and psychology, and so on down the line to basket weaving. You can readily reflect on your undergraduate education to assess how rigorous it has been; the admissions committee will probably come up with a similar or more critical evaluation.

Most admissions committees will examine in detail the specific courses you have completed. In some instances, the committee will require the completion of specific courses, such as organic chemistry for medical school. When there is a firm requirement that specific courses be completed, this will be stated in the bulletin of the program.

You may be required to demonstrate competence in certain subject areas through good grades in specific courses or areas of study.

Even when there are no specific courses that must be completed prior to admission, the program may look for success in certain disciplines or areas of study. For example, an M.B.A. program may assess whether an applicant has completed economics or statistics courses. These courses may also be used as an indicator of your potential for success in similar graduate coursework. It is important to keep this in mind because a relatively weak application can be strengthened by the elective completion of additional rigorous courses—this sends a positive message concerning your abilities to the admissions committee.

In the final analysis grades are almost always the most important criterion for admission—every applicant must face this reality.

And finally, the dreaded truth is that it is grades, above all other factors, that are usually most carefully examined by a critical admissions committee as the most important decision criterion. There is certainly a lot of controversy concerning grades. Some people feel that grades are a poor indication of native intelligence. Others believe that lots of people's undergraduate grades are hurt by the good times that they had in college. Still others think that grades fail to capture motivation and interest in advanced study, factors that will have a lot to do with success in graduate or professional school. In the final analysis, however, these rather theoretical concerns have little impact on the plain truth of the matter. Grades are nearly always the single most important component of an applicant's admissions credentials. There is no way to ignore or play down this factor. About the only exception to this rule is in the arts, where talent may supersede pure academic performance.

To understand the importance of grades, you need to understand what the admissions committee sees in them. First and foremost they are read as an indicator of a student's success in an academic environment. The admissions committee seeks to admit people who will do well, or at least will not do poorly, in meeting the scholastic requirements of graduate or professional education. Grades are also considered to reflect an applicant's determination, commitment, and seriousness as a student. Finally, grades provide insight into fundamental intellectual ability. By examining how well a student has done in different fields, an admissions committee can determine the applicant's relative strengths and weaknesses. This information provides some insight into the academic areas in which you are likely to do well or poorly. Good grades in different areas will suggest that you are an adaptable person able to conquer almost any challenge.

Not all grades are created equal—your grades in some areas of study will be much more important than those in other areas.

Your best grades should be in those areas of study that are most germane to the field you are applying for. This is especially important because most students earn some good and some not-so-good grades in college; it is very important which courses have the best grades. It is common knowledge, for example, that an applicant to medical school had better have high grades in science courses; a weak course grade in history or the arts will likely be far less damaging than one in organic chemistry.

If you are reading this book in the freshman or sophomore years of college, you have ample time to accumulate outstanding grades suitable for admission to graduate or professional school. If not, you should immediately obtain and carefully examine a copy of your college transcript. List all of your courses on a sheet of paper according to grade. All of the courses in which you received an A or its equivalent should be listed in one column, the B courses in the next, and so forth, as low as is necessary to go in the grading scale. Then look at the courses in each of the columns and determine if you have any notable groupings. For example, are your best grades, especially in the A column, earned in science or mathematics, or art courses? If you can identify consistent patterns of grades by area of study, you will be in a strong position to know your areas of acceptable performance and your weak subject areas. The admissions committee will essentially do the same thing.

If your strengths turn out to be different from the subject areas required in your proposed program, you have a problem. You can either change your chosen field or address your deficiencies in your application.

The harder the courses and the better your grades, the more impressive will be your credentials.

As noted above, grades are the single most important factor in the consideration of your application for admission. But a grade is not a grade is not a grade. A grade in a "soft" course may not count as much as the same grade in a "hard" course. The relative value of a grade depends, of course, on the specific program to which you are applying. You might consider asking the program which courses are most important in the admissions-review process. This type of information is generally available, and can be very valuable in assessing your own credentials.

While you should always strive for good grades in every course, you should strive extra hard in your more difficult courses. Courses that reflect on your intellectual ability or aptitudes are especially important.

Most admissions committees are adept at determining the level of sophistication of the courses you have completed. Only in rare instances will you be able to pull the wool over the eyes of the seasoned faculty members who sit on the admissions committees. Taking a course at a more advanced level and doing well will almost always count more than taking the same subject matter at a more basic level. Even if the course names sound similar, the more advanced or rigorous courses will almost always be detected by the admissions committee, and will be given more weight.

Avoid bad grades, especially in important courses relevant to your proposed area of study.

Most admissions committees, although not all, will examine the last two years of academic performance much more carefully than the first two years. It is often assumed that the first two years contain easier courses, that the student is using this time to adjust to college, and that freshmen and sophomores are less serious in the pursuit of their studies. The last two years are, on the other hand, more advanced, require more dedication, and are completed with the awareness that graduation is approaching. Bad grades, if you have any, will hurt you less if they were earned during the first two years of study.

A bad grade, by the way, potentially includes anything below an A, especially in these days of grade inflation. Grades earned before the early 1970s probably have more weight attached to them because grading in college was generally more difficult in those days. However, an applicant seeking to attend graduate or professional school who has been out in the working world for a number of years may be at a disadvantage. Since the older transcripts will contain grades earned when grading was more stringent, the newer graduate may look better on paper than someone who graduated a number of years ago. While many admissions committees take this into account indirectly, it is very difficult to adequately adjust these older grades. As a result, there is little that can be done quantitatively to compare the old with the new, and the lower grade—even if awarded when it was really hard to earn an "A"—will look worse. In addition, the older applicants will often do worse on standardized tests, since they have been out of school for a while.

The problem of grade inflation is serious. Many people sail through college these days with what appear to be very good grades. But when looked at carefully, the grades may be vastly inflated from what they would have been ten or twelve years ago. To deal with this situation, admissions committees consider other factors such as the types and levels of courses completed, the school from which the grades were earned, the difficulty of the undergraduate program, and, of course, the results of standardized tests.

Separate grade-point averages may be computed for various categories of courses completed.

Most programs will compute your undergraduate grade-point average (GPA). Depending on the needs of the admissions committee, averages may also be computed for specific groups of courses, such as all of your science courses. In addition, a separate GPA may be computed for the last two years of college work. Another grade-point average may be computed for the harder courses you completed or for those in selected disciplines or fields of study. There are indeed many different computations that can be performed. Many of these are designed to eliminate from consideration easy courses, early undergraduate performance, and irrelevant coursework.

If you attended a college where grades were not awarded, you could be at a disadvantage in competing for an acceptance.

An interesting problem arises in the computation of grade-point averages for students who don't have any grades. In the academic turmoil of the late 1960s and early 1970s some schools did away with grades. And some of these schools were quite good academic institutions. Instead of grades, the transcript consists of statement after statement of instructor assessments about the student's performance in class. These transcripts can continue for many pages. While these schools are creative and innovative and should be applauded for trying something new, they can do a disservice to their students.

The absence of grades is rarely beneficial to the students and can put them at a competitive disadvantage. If all other things were equal, most graduate or professional schools would probably accept a student with grades before one without grades. For one thing, students without grades cannot be easily compared to students with grades. With no grade-point average to compute, there is little ability to summarize quantitatively the student's academic ability.

The ungraded transcript usually extends to page after page of qualitative comments from various instructors. A student takes a lot of courses in college. The time it takes to read such a transcript is far in excess of the time required to review a traditional list of grades. As a result, the comments of many of your instructors may be read only very briefly, if at all. What's worse, these transcripts do not prioritize information, so that the more important comments from instructors who knew you better, such as those reflecting a perceptive understanding of your abilities, are lost in the pages of comments. Although there is certainly a lot wrong with grades, in most instances they do reflect a student's relative academic performance. A transcript consisting only of comments lacks adequate relative-performance information, so that the admissions committee cannot judge whether or not you did well based on superficially pleasant comments from an instructor. And just as there has been grade inflation, many professors are reluctant to put negative comments in writing.

If you don't have grades, you can expect other factors, such as standardized test scores, to be weighed more heavily.

Don't let the absence of grades instill in you a false sense of security. If you are stuck with a transcript that doesn't use grades, you can expect the admissions committee to take an especially critical look at your standardized test scores, at the college and program attended, and at the field of study at the undergraduate level. You might even want to take a couple of difficult graduate-level courses at another institution to obtain a few good grades.

Memberships in honorary societies, academic awards, and other evidence of scholastic achievement can be very beneficial to an applicant.

There is another potentially powerful indicator of academic performance, in the form of memberships in honorary societies. The most famous and impressive of these is Phi Beta Kappa. There are many others, of course, including some in professional fields. These societies admit only the top performers in each class, at least in theory, and use selection criteria similar to that used by admissions committees. And the more prestigious and selective the honorary society, the better.

The completion, with good grades, of some rigorous graduate-level courses will help demonstrate your academic abilities.

Some applicants will have completed graduate-level coursework prior to applying to graduate school, either while still an undergraduate, in the process of attending another graduate or professional degree program, or simply as the result of having taken some postgraduate courses after college. Undergraduates are commonly allowed to complete some graduate courses, often in their junior or senior years.

The completion of graduate courses by an undergraduate is not in itself very impressive to the admissions committee. However, if you do well in a number of graduate-level courses, especially if they are difficult courses, the admissions committee will know that you are able to handle coursework at this level.

A student who has completed all or part of a graduate-degree program prior to applying to another program will have to submit a transcript for the courses completed. This will be viewed by the admissions committee differently than they view an undergraduate transcript. Graduate courses are usually graded more leniently or on a different scale from undergraduate courses. Before grade inflation became as severe as it has been in recent years, grades at the undergraduate level were usually pegged to an average grade of C, while at the graduate level the average has been a B. In addition, the minimum grade-point average required for graduation frequently is B, or 3.0 or its equivalent, at the graduate level. Thus, undergraduate and graduate courses and grades are not strictly comparable.

In assessing your prior graduate work, if any, the program will be interested in why you started and why you did not complete another program. If you have completed a graduate or professional program and are now seeking admission to a program in a different field, the admissions committee will be interested in your rationale for the change. These concerns should be addressed in the interview and narrative statements submitted with the application.

Jumping around between graduate and professional programs, and poor prior grades at the graduate level, will have to be explained.

The admissions committee will obviously look at graduate-level performance with a critical eye. An applicant with poor performance at the graduate level can be at a significant disadvantage. On the other hand, good grades in relatively difficult graduate-level courses is an important plus.

At both the undergraduate and graduate levels there are few firm rules for determining the "minimum" grade-point average that is needed for admission. Many factors are examined, and many trade-offs are made. However, you should be able to obtain from the program the average, mean, or median grade-point average for applicants accepted in the prior year. In addition, you may be able to obtain both the minimum average that is recommended and the range of actual averages for last year's entering class. This information should help you determine where you stand in the applicant pool. Appendix A is designed to help you compare data for various schools.

A transcript that contains a lot of incomplete grades, withdrawals from courses, and audits is also suspect. There is a tendency to view such a record as reflecting a lack of commitment, as an attempt to avoid hard courses, and as a means of protecting the transcript from low grades. Remember that even these "nongrades" will be examined to provide insight into the type of student you are.

A few bad grades may not be fatal unless they are in critical required courses.

Not every applicant has stellar grades. Many people have one or two "bad" grades, generally anything below a B or a 3.0. If these are not in critical courses, and if there is adequate evidence of academic ability or potential from other grades and standardized test scores, these few bad grades will probably be overlooked. They will, however, always stand out on your transcript.

For the student with a less-than-impressive transcript, more overt action may be required to overcome the negative effects of bad grades. Admission to graduate or professional school is a competitive process that weighs all applicants, one against the other. The more selective the school or program, the more competitive an applicant must be to succeed in gaining admission. In especially competitive programs it is not uncommon for a grade-point average below 3.5 or 3.6 to be considered representative of poor undergraduate performance. If you have what appear to be poor grades, something else will be needed to strengthen your application. Also, your grade performance will be compared with the results of standardized tests, which then become very important. Poor performance on the tests could be a fatal blow to your application.

You can partially offset bad grades by achieving high grades in difficult, graduate-level courses that are relevant to your proposed program.

There are not all that many ways to strengthen your application that will overcome poor grades, especially once you have completed college. After all, you spent four or five years accumulating your record. However, the best way to demonstrate your academic ability is probably through the completion of additional coursework. You should enroll for advanced undergraduate or graduate-level courses that serve as good preparation for your proposed field of study. For example, an applicant to business school might take graduate-level courses in economics, while an applicant to a doctoral program in experimental psychology might take advanced courses in statistics.

The completion of graduate courses with high grades, preferably very high grades, can impress the admissions committee. However, the courses should be rigorous and as advanced as possible. They should also be taken from a university of recognized high quality. Finally, they should, when possible, be regular daytime graduate courses taken by full-time students. Courses in evening programs, extended-degree programs, and special courses for nonmajors will often be discounted by the admissions committee. In addition, courses from weak schools will have far less impact than difficult courses from well-known institutions. The programs to which you are applying will probably be able to advise you concerning which courses, universities, and fields of study are worthwhile, both in terms of providing good preparation for advanced study and of strengthening your application.

But the bottom line is that every student and every applicant should always keep in mind the importance of grades throughout all of their years of preparation.

CHAPTER 8 *Coping with Standardized Tests*

THE MOST AWESOME PART of the admissions process for many people, including some of the brightest and most confident applicants, is the frequent requirement to take standardized tests. The best known of these tests is probably the Graduate Record Examination. The Medical College Admission Test, Graduate Management Admission Test, and Law School Admission Test are among the other exams that cause applicants endless worry and concern. Few applicants, however, understand how the tests are actually used and the extent to which they are an important part of the admissions decision.

Few people like test scores, but most admissions committees still feel they are essential factors to be considered.

Standardized tests are designed primarily to measure aptitude. The underlying purpose of both grades and test scores is to predict success in graduate or professional school. The admissions committee seeks to accept students who will not only be able to complete the program of study successfully but will also be able to do well in the field of practice. Unfortunately, academic success is often difficult to predict. This is especially true because of the very wide diversity in backgrounds of the applicants. If everyone attended the same college, had the same major, and exhibited the same degree of motivation, then prediction of success could probably be based almost solely on grades, and the results would, in all likelihood, be pretty good. But this is not realistic.

Amazingly, few people on either side of the fence, applicants or faculty, are happy with standardized tests. There are many inequities and inaccuracies associated with these tests, which must be viewed with extreme caution. But there are also few programs and schools that are willing to ignore test results, since they need to obtain quantitative data on which to make the admissions decision.

Standardized tests have been controversial for a long time. They have been accused of being culturally biased, of not measuring academic potential, of favoring the quick rather than the deep and careful thinker, and of many other sins. Probably many of these accusations are at least partially valid.

There are a number of approaches to using standardized tests that are common among admissions committees. Unfortunately, some schools and programs use test scores and grades to compute an automatic cutoff for admissions consideration. Thus, a student without a minimum combination of both test scores and grades is automatically excluded from further consideration. Since there is a trade-off between grades, which measure prior performance, and test scores, which measure academic potential, most admissions committees use the combination of both to determine potential academic success. The actual quantitative measures may be combined through an algebraic computation to yield a total "prediction score." Anyone who fails to meet the minimum total prediction score may be excluded, and large numbers of applications can be given a preliminary review this way. In many instances factors such as undergraduate major, school attended, and other graduate courses may also be factored into the equation.

Test scores, when used with grades and other factors, probably are useful predictors of academic, although not necessarily professional, success.

There is some evidence that a predictive equation can be used successfully, at least in part, to determine who should be accepted at the graduate level. Studies of students in some fields such as medicine and management have demonstrated that students with more rigorous undergraduate training, with higher undergraduate grades, and with higher standardized tests scores, especially in the quantitative and analytical areas, do better in rigorous, academically oriented graduate and professional programs. These results are probably intuitively obvious, especially with respect to undergraduate grades. Thus, a candidate who does not have either strong grades or good test scores has a serious problem.

Test scores ignore many other factors that are associated with success in the classroom and, more importantly, in a career.

Do test scores actually predict success? The analytical studies that have been completed indicate that they do. But —and this is a big but—there are probably many students who can succeed in graduate school and in the professions but who do not perform well on standardized tests. If they are automatically excluded, they lose a chance to achieve what they may in fact be quite capable of achieving. Furthermore, the argument is often made that outstanding grades in graduate and professional programs are not the same as outstanding performance in a career. Thus, while someone may do well in the classroom, he or she may not do well in a career, especially since the skills required in the classroom and those needed in the field of practice may be very different. Many students who squeak through school have outstanding careers.

Thus, the dilemma that the admissions committee faces in the use of standardized tests is extremely complex. While many applicants are distrustful and concerned by the use of these tests because they may measure the wrong things or are not accurate measures of academic potential, the admissions committee needs them as indicators of success that can validate their decision-making process.

Standardized test scores can be a savior for students with relatively low grades or other credentials problems.

There is a brighter side to the standardized test picture. For applicants without strong grades, the standardized test essentially offers an opportunity for reprieve, a chance to demonstrate academic potential. If grades were the sole predictor of performance used for admissions, many students would be eliminated. There are those who suffer through a slow start in college for a variety of reasons, ranging from poor study habits to preferring to have a good time for a couple of years after leaving the nest. These individuals may never fully rescue their academic record when they finally become serious and successful students. If you fall into this category, standardized tests offer you another avenue for demonstrating your potential as a graduate student. Of course, you are also faced with demonstrating your commitment to serious study, given the lack of it at the undergraduate level. This can be done through accumulating good grades during the last couple of years of college, through an impressive interview or narrative statement, and through other evidence that shows your serious side.

Exactly how standardized tests are used by each admissions committee can vary substantially. While some committees use them initially to screen out all candidates who do not have at least a minimum level of academic potential, this is far from the full story. Every applicant should be aware that in most cases grades are more important than test scores. After all, you spend four or more years accumulating an academic record, while test scores are usually the result of one day's effort.

Test scores are primarily used to measure intelligence, and sometimes knowledge, and most of the tests are basically similar to each other.

Test scores are often taken as a measure of intelligence. The higher the test scores, the higher the level of implied intelligence—hence, the greater the success potential of the applicant. Most standardized tests are similar, although specific sections differ substantially, each being adapted for a particular field or type of advanced study. A few, such as Miller's Analogy, are substantially different from the rest. For the most part a student will likely score in a comparable range on more than one of the standardized tests, and some programs will even accept more than one test for their requirement.

While many of the tests have questions of knowledge on specific topics, the tests are not used, generally speaking, to measure your knowledge of subjects, except for the advanced knowledge tests of the Graduate Record Examination and certain parts of other exams. Indeed, most members of admissions committees would probably be hard-pressed to tell you what types of questions and what specific areas are covered on the examinations. Many faculty haven't even seen a test sample in years.

The test's questions relating to your subject-area knowledge are only a foil. The true objective is usually to discern your thinking ability, generally in three types of skills. The first is verbal ability, or facility with communication, word use, comprehension, and the like. The second area of testing is quantitative ability, or the ability to think in terms of numbers, mathematical relationships, and so forth. The last area of concern is analytical ability, or the ability to think and to reason, to understand and analyze situations, and to draw conclusions. Of course, each test has its own specific objectives and orientations, the details of which are spelled out in information that is widely available.

Programs use tests to determine a student's intellectual potential in the specific areas that are emphasized in their curriculum. A program in engineering will emphasize the quantitative measures more than the verbal ones; an English program will pay more attention to the verbal scores. Many programs, especially in professional fields, prefer a well-rounded student, and to ensure breadth of intelligence most programs will also want to see at least minimally respectable scores on all parts of the tests.

Your exact test score is less important than the range or percentile that your score falls into—you want to be in the top percentiles.

Most programs recognize the inexact nature of test scores and their failure to pinpoint intellectual ability accurately and consistently. As a result, most programs will not use your exact score as a definitive measure of academic potential. Rather, it is the range or percentile within which the score lies that is important. Scores can usually move up or down within at least a twenty-point range in either direction and still fall within one standard deviation, and many committees will use the percentile or approximate range of the score in assessing applicants. Thus, two students with scores within twenty or thirty points of each other are pretty much identical in terms of test results. Of course, unless the evaluation is done on a computer, there is still a human element that may attribute greater potential to the applicant with the higher score regardless of the statistical relevance of doing so. One can only hope this does not occur too often.

Some programs also use the reported percentile ranking rather than the actual score. The percentile, which is also

Coping with Standardized Tests

reported to the applicant on most test report forms, simply reflects how an applicant scored in comparison to all of the individuals who took the test over a specified time span. This comparison is particularly useful for a program that has a good feel for the percentile scores of applicants they usually attract or the percentile scores that are associated with students who succeed in the program. Again, there may be preferences for higher verbal or quantitative percentile results, depending on the field.

Since the analytical component of the Graduate Record Examination is relatively new, it is used less than the verbal and quantitative scores. Remember that the school or program has no control over the exam other than to require that an applicant take one.

Some schools require that applicants take advanced knowledge tests in addition to the aptitude tests. These are especially useful in graduate programs where prior knowledge of a subject matter is essential, especially in doctoral programs. The advanced knowledge tests are more a measure of an individual's actual knowledge and abilities than of aptitudes.

Care should be taken in deciding whether to have multiple results of the same test reported, and even whether to take a test more than once.

In some instances an applicant who has taken a standardized test more than once can request that only one set of scores be reported to the program. Obviously you want to report the best scores that you have attained. In some circumstances the scores for each time that you took the test will be automatically reported to the programs. This may present a problem.

Most people who take a standardized test more than once do so to improve their scores. Only rarely do the scores come out the same when a candidate takes a test multiple times. If the scores are very close, the admissions committee will likely take them as a fairly firm measure of your aptitude. Since there would be little point in taking a test more than once if your first scores were high, you probably are trying to improve your score. But a second low score would present an unfortunate situation.

Many programs will give you the benefit of the doubt and use your higher test scores if multiple test results are reported.

If multiple test scores are reported to the schools and one set is substantially better than the other, many programs will use the higher results. This can be very important and you might want to ask the program about its policy on this. In some situations scores may be averaged while in others the most recent score may be used; in both cases one might not want to take the test a second or third time.

There are a few other strategies you can consider, although they are somewhat farfetched. The first of these is to have the initial scores reported to the school automatically after you have taken the test. If these scores are relatively low, retake the test quickly but have the new scores reported only after you see them and have determined that they are an improvement. If they are worse, you need do nothing with them, and the program will never know that you took the test again. This strategy requires good timing and a little advance planning.

Another alternative is to take a different standardized test. In some fields programs will accept more than one type of test. The applicant can simply take two different tests and have only the scores of the best test sent to the program. Again, this requires some advance planning, since you will not be able to have the scores sent to the schools at the time the test is taken. There are also some additional costs involved, although they are minor.

Finally, the most drastic approach is to bring your applicant's test score report to the program personally. If the first set of test results is higher than any subsequent retesting, ask the program personnel if they will accept your copy of the first set of results. If they do, they need never see the later test scores. However, many programs require an original report form from the testing agency, and so this ploy is not likely to work in these situations. One variation on this strategy is to hand the program secretary the first results, and say that you will arrange to have an official copy sent later. Then wait and have the official copy sent to the program after you are accepted.

Whether it is to your advantage to retake standardized tests to try to improve your scores depends on a number of complex factors and requires a judgment on your part.

The issue of candidates taking standardized tests multiple times is highly controversial. Everyone seems to have advice on the topic. Official pronouncements often are confusing and misleading. The bottom line is that, on the average, candidates who take the tests multiple times do improve their scores. However, those who retake the tests are a selected group; many of them may not have felt well when they initially took the test, or they may have other nonintellectual reasons for an earlier poor performance. In addition, while some individuals do attain substantially higher scores, the average gain on retakes is only about twenty-five points, which may be too little a gain to justify the cost and time involved in the retake.

Whether it is worthwhile to retake any of these examinations is dependent on two factors: how well you scored initially, and the range of desirable scores for the program that you seek to enter. Most people have taken other standardized tests, such as the SAT, before seeking admission to graduate or professional schools. You should know how well you usually do on these measures of aptitude from your past experience. The testing philosophy, with the exception of the GRE Advanced Knowledge Test, is generally similar for most tests. Someone who consistently does poorly on standardized tests is unlikely to improve significantly. On the other hand, someone who usually does well will more than likely do well again. If you take the standardized tests and do fairly well, or at least score at or above the median of those previously accepted into the program you seek to enter, you will probably not want to take them again. On the other hand, if you score below the median but usually do well on the tests, you may benefit from a retake. If you scored low but usually do poorly on these types of tests, you may want to retake them even though the odds are not especially favorable for doing well on a retake. Finally, if you scored fairly well but usually do not do well on standardized tests, count your blessings and quit while you are ahead.

Low test scores can be partially offset, to a point, by other positive credentials and especially by good grades.

Since most programs use standardized tests in conjunction with other admissions criteria, it is actually the combination of factors that is important—especially the combination of test scores and grades. One of the essential points of this book is that applicants should seek to strengthen each aspect of their credentials in order to maximize their chances of admission. For example, relatively low test scores can, up to a point, be at least partially offset by good grades, especially by those earned in difficult subjects. Hence the importance of working hard in college.

Test preparation courses may be useful, especially for individuals who have difficulty with standardized tests.

There is also considerable controversy about the value of taking special cram courses that are offered around the country to prepare students for a wide variety of standardized tests.

These courses may or may not pay off in higher test results, but they are probably useful for individuals who have difficulty taking standardized tests. The experience of working through sample exercises and of understanding the testing process a little better can pay off. Whether or not you should take these courses requires a little cost-benefit analysis and personal judgment. If you are really cautious, you may want to play it safe by taking advantage of any opportunity to improve your chances of admission.

Most programs require that an applicant have taken a standardized test within a certain period of time prior to applying, often five years. Test scores are compared to the cohort of other applicants taking the test over the past few years. Therefore, changes over time in the composition of the group taking the test can affect how one applicant does in relation to other applicants. This is why the admissions committee prefers to have everyone take the test within the same time span. This presents problems for some people, however.

Applicants who have worked for a number of years after college and who then seek admission to graduate or professional school may not do as well on standardized tests as they would have on tests taken right after graduating from college. The effect of a rigorous college program on honing one's academic skills is difficult to measure, but you could be at some disadvantage after working for a few years, especially on the quantitative parts of the test, unless you have a particularly rigorous, academically oriented job. If you are now completing college and expect to work for a few years before going on to graduate or professional school, you might want to take your standardized tests now as a form of protection. This assumes that you know what field you will be seeking to enter, of course. And doing so certainly does not preclude taking the tests again when preparing to apply for graduate school.

Minority students often have difficulty with standardized tests for a variety of reasons, but they also frequently receive special consideration.

Minority students may also experience some difficulty with standardized tests and would do well to consider preparing in advance for such tests through special courses or instructional books; however, minorities will sometimes receive special consideration by the admissions committee with regard to test scores. The minority applicant can ask the program the range and median for all the accepted students and for minority acceptances during the past year. This information should provide some indication of whether any special consideration is given to minority applicants. Foreign students may experience even more severe difficulties. The Test of English as a Foreign Language is usually required for foreign students, and individual programs may have a mandatory cutoff score.

Test scores are a reality that is here to stay, but they are only one of many factors in the admissions decision.

Test scores are rarely used alone. The most serious situation is when a program has an automatic test score cutoff below which no candidate will be considered. There is little that the applicant can do about this policy except to apply elsewhere or retake the examination. However, test scores are almost always used in conjunction with other credentials, especially grades.

There are a number of complex statistical issues related to standardized tests that are interesting but of little practical value to the applicant. The use, validity, reliability, and biases of these tests are constantly debated by faculty. Applicants who do well on the tests usually don't object, and those who do poorly regularly complain that the tests do not reflect their abilities. But the tests continue to be used and are likely to be used in the future.

CHAPTER 9 *Your Experience and Background*

WHILE THE MOST IMPORTANT FACTORS in the acceptance decision are, unquestionably, your academic performance and potential, other factors also may loom large. Especially in professional programs, your experience and other background credentials can be of considerable importance. Of course these additional factors of themselves will rarely override poor performance, but they can at least partially help to offset below-average academic credentials.

Your background and experience reflect exposure to the profession, maturity, interests, and personal accomplishments.

You should understand why admissions committees look at experience and background issues. The most important reasons that these factors are considered at all are that they reflect your past exposure to the field you want to enter and reflect your maturity, personal development, and the scope of your interests and accomplishments.

In terms of exposure to your potential professional field, practical experience tells the admissions committee that you have some knowledge and understanding of what you are getting into. This is important because, especially in professional programs, the faculty want to accept individuals for advanced study who are sure of the path they are following. The faculty will be investing time and effort in each and every student. They want to make this investment in people who will stay in the program through graduation, and who will establish and maintain careers in the field for which they have been trained.

Your experience can help the admissions committee feel confident that you know what you are getting into.

Accepting students who have a commitment to the field of practice has value for the faculty beyond considerations of ego. Students who enter a program but do not graduate reflect badly on the program in a number of respects. First, they reduce the number of program graduates, a number that is often used to measure the faculty's success in education. Second, students who do not graduate are often unhappy and do not contribute to the good reputation of the program. And third, students who graduate and are employed form an alumni network that the faculty can rely upon to support the program through job placement, through the development of the program's reputation, through student field training, and in the recruitment of additional faculty and students.

Experience suggests exposure to the field, maturity, and commitment.

Understood in the context of such issues as commitment and future contributions to the field of practice, you can appreciate why faculty want indications that applicants will follow through both in the training program and in the field of practice. While a few dropouts always are expected, most programs want to minimize this number. Thus, if your experience and other indicators of commitment demonstrate an unusually high likelihood of your pursuing the field of practice, you are more likely to be favorably viewed by the admissions committee.

The other major perspective on background information is the extent to which it reflects an applicant's maturity. Applicants with full-time experience are older and often more mature. Many professional programs, especially, appreciate the seasoning that occurs through an applicant's work experience. Some programs will accept only people who have full-time work experience, under the assumption that this leads to a classroom composed of individuals who are serious, have an understanding of their intended field of practice, and are especially interested in their studies. This last issue is of particular interest.

In many professional fields students with experience are easier and more fun to teach.

In many professional programs students who have experience are not only more interesting to teach but better able to contribute to classroom discussion. Experienced students can bring their experience into the classroom to the benefit of both the faculty and the other students. In addition, they can mentally relate issues and topics discussed by the faculty to what they have seen occur in the so-called real world. The student can bridge the field of practice and the academic setting of the classroom. Of course, this only applies to certain fields, such as business management. In other fields, such as law, medicine, or dentistry, the relationship between the profession, as the student may have seen it, and the classroom is far less important and direct. On the other hand, these programs still want applicants who have an understanding of what they are getting into and who are committed to the field. Thus, the importance the admissions committee places on prior experience varies considerably.

In more technical fields admissions committees are likely to be biased toward the "brainy" applicant, while in the applied fields maturity and experience are important.

Many programs must choose between admitting younger, academically oriented students with little or no practical exposure and older, academically less well-prepared but more mature students. The choice between these alternatives will largely depend on the field and the biases of the faculty. In more academically rigorous programs, such as medicine or engineering, the bias will likely be toward the more academic, cerebral applicant who has outstanding grades and test scores but less experience. In the more applied fields, such as business administration or law, the emphasis will be more oriented toward the mature and experienced student. In recent years the academic rigor of most programs in all fields has increased so that there is now probably more concern with, and increased bias toward, the academically well-prepared student. For example, the better business administration programs now include required coursework in quantitative methods, for which students must have the aptitude to handle statistics, operations research, and other quantitative material.

Older, more mature students are more interesting and, in some fields, are easier to place in jobs.

Experience also leads to other attributes or dimensions of an applicant that someone right out of an undergraduate program frequently lacks. In many fields an individual who has no experience is harder for the faculty to place when it comes time to assist students in finding jobs. Also, the faculty more often enjoy students who are mature, have experience, and who can be treated more as colleagues. But again, this varies from field to field.

In relatively academic graduate fields experience may be of limited value. In these instances laboratory or research-assistant experience might be taken either as an indication that you are willing to work in the trenches or as evidence that you may be a great scientist in the making.

In other fields, such as medicine or law, in which the program wants to "mold" the student into the faculty's image of the ideal practitioner through professional socialization, there is also likely to be little interest in the applicant with extensive experience. Experience in this type of situation should reflect exposure to the profession, commitment to the field, and a willingness to work hard.

In some fields the admissions committee will be interested in the details of your work experience; in others the committee will only superficially look at this information.

Some admissions committees, especially in applied professional fields, will be very interested in the specific substance of your experience. How much responsibility have you had? What was the level or complexity of the jobs you held? What is your potential for upward mobility? This type of information can be very important in the admissions decision and may partially offset less-than-competitive academic performance.

Your experience should be honestly reflected in the application materials, but you should also ensure that all relevant information is included. Many application forms provide precious little physical space for you to list and explain your complete experience and background.

Do whatever is necessary to include adequate detail about your experience, and try to make your background sound as impressive as possible without misrepresenting yourself.

An applicant with impressive experience will probably want to add supplemental pages to the application whenever possible. But you should also keep in mind that the members of the admissions committee are extremely busy and you should not use excessive verbiage or unnecessary explanations.

Experience that you want to emphasize can be included in a supplemental statement that lists your experience and the dates during which you were employed. You should indicate whether the experience was full-time or part-time and whether it was salaried or voluntary. This can be done easily, using either a simplified résumé or, as noted above, supplemental pages added to the application forms.

It is generally not necessary to list your experience on both a supplemental sheet and the application form. If you use supplemental sheets, you can probably write "see supplemental sheet," or something to this effect, in the area of the application forms reserved for listing your experience.

If you do provide further information about your background than what is routinely requested, you should make it clear why you are including this material. For example, accomplishments in the arts or in languages may reflect both your perseverance and your intelligence. Present this information in a manner that shows that you are an exceptional applicant. Think about the information from the perspective of the admissions committee. Draft a supplemental statement and show it to friends or faculty advisers for their opinions.

There is also a negative side to supplemental information. Any added information in your application increases the time it takes members of the admissions committee to read your file. An unduly long file may lead to some resentment on the part of faculty members, who may resist having to allocate undue time to review it. Therefore, be sure that added information is relevant and concisely presented.

Do not put unnecessary and extraneous filler material in your application.

Some applicants also provide what might be termed "filler" material with their applications. For example, if you published a journal article, you might want to include it. It may or may not be read, but it will look impressive and can readily be

Your Experience and Background

ignored by those members of the committee who are not interested in spending time reading it. On the other hand, pages and pages of typed manuscript material are unlikely to be read and simply increase the bulk of the admissions file without really adding to the substance. Only include material that is truly of such importance that it should be brought to the attention of the admissions committee.

You want to assure the admissions committee that you know what you are getting into, that you are committed to the training program and to the field of practice, and that you will work hard and are willing to pay your dues.

CHAPTER 10 *The Interview and How to Handle It*

To MOST APPLICANTS TO GRADUATE and professional schools the interview is the most threatening aspect of the admissions process. And for good reason. While grades and test scores and most of the other evidence used to judge applicants are relatively objective, the interview allows for many opportunities to introduce bias and discrimination. Applicants are justifiably concerned about the interview and should make every effort to ensure that, if there is one, it goes smoothly. As discussed in this chapter, however, the interview can also be a positive opportunity for some people who might otherwise stand little or no chance for admission.

The interview is an opportunity for the program to judge you, and vice versa.

Not all schools require, request, or even allow interviews. And the nature and function of the interview can vary widely. You should be aware that the interview has two main purposes. The first is the more obvious one of assessing characteristics of an applicant that are not available from other documentation. This is a major reason for personal interviews, especially where there is extreme competition for admission, such as in medical schools.

The second, more benign, reason for interviews, which may surprise some applicants, is to sell the school to the student. This is especially useful when there are too few applicants for the available positions or when there are many applicants but relatively few good ones. It may be quite difficult for you to discern whether you are being interviewed to add subjective information about you to the admissions file, or to impress you as a particularly desirable applicant that the program wants to recruit. It is wise, however, unless you have extremely attractive credentials and no skeletons in the closet, or are especially cocky, to assume that you are being interviewed so that the school can gain further information and insight into your strengths and weaknesses.

Interviews are subjective, potentially biased and discriminatory, and may reveal your personal behavior and attitudes.

The bad news about interviews is that as much as they may be designed to determine relatively legitimate and objective information, such as your career goals, they also inevitably reveal your physical appearance, personality, and interpersonal abilities. Regardless of disclaimers to the contrary, these factors may indeed be taken into consideration in the admissions decision, to the detriment of some applicants. On the other hand, you may strengthen an otherwise weak set of credentials with an outstanding performance that reflects unusual poise, charm, knowledge, and commitment.

Again, not all schools require interviews, and there is frequently not even any great degree of consistency within each professional field. There are some fields, however, such as medicine and dentistry, where the absence of an interview would be unusual. In instances where an interview is clearly a requirement, you should not attempt to avoid complying unless the most extreme circumstances prevail. Admissions committees will often prefer the known quantity to the unknown.

You may want to try to avoid an interview if you are likely to leave a bad impression.

In general, you will not want to be interviewed if you are likely to make a bad impression. Thus, if you make every effort to impress people but still uniformly fail to do so, then you are unlikely to benefit from the interview under any circumstances; you may even damage your cause. There is, of course, an exception even to this rule. If your references imply personality difficulties or lack of communication skills, it may still be to your benefit to counteract this negative information by proving, through an interview, that you are not a complete ogre. Thus, you must carefully weigh the situation and consider the advice that follows as well.

There are legitimate excuses for not being able to participate in an interview.

You may also have some legitimate reasons for not being able to comply with the request for an interview. This may include severe illness—which, by the way, you should indicate will not affect your ability to report for school. Another reason for not being interviewed may be that you live too far from the proposed site of the interview. This may be a legitimate reason for politely suggesting that an interview would impose severe hardships. Travel expenses or time required for traveling to the interview site may be very real problems. However, in dealing with such a situation you must be cautious not to imply that this school is so low on your priority list that you prefer to use your money to go skiing, or that you just don't want to bother with an interview. Faculties are very sensitive.

If travel is indeed a problem, you should frankly communicate this to the admissions people. You generally will meet with some sympathy, since high airfares and travel costs are familiar to everyone. Some schools will accommodate you, but others may be less willing to do so. The school will always be attempting to gauge whether your inability to appear for an interview is an indication of true financial difficulties or lack of interest. The admissions committee may even examine related evidence such as where you live, what your parents do, or summer job experiences to obtain a hint as to the degree to which you are avoiding them because of genuine financial hardship.

If you are avoiding an interview, be honest but careful in what you reveal about yourself.

If you have a handicap or other legitimate reason for refusing the invitation to interview, you should be relatively honest about your situation. But you should put things in a positive light. While most committees will try to avoid any form of discrimination, there is also a normal psychological process by which information cannot be readily ignored once it is learned. Thus, what you are willing to reveal about yourself should be carefully thought out.

Handicapped candidates should impress the committee with their professionalism, obvious ability to overcome, and commitment to advanced study.

A handicapped individual might want to point out that the combination of travel costs and the handicap would make an interview difficult, although attending school would, of course, present no insurmountable problems. The handicapped student may make a particularly positive impression, since most faculty members are sensitive and especially attuned to a professional-appearing performance by anyone. In some situations, such as medical and dental schools, detailed information on the type of handicap must be provided, and no effort to conceal or misrepresent is justifiable. In other situations it is essential to assure the committee that you can successfully meet the academic and physical rigor of graduate study. The successful completion of an undergraduate education is surely solid evidence of your abilities. And a letter of reference that points out your enthusiasm, drive, and commitment certainly cannot hurt.

Do not reveal information about yourself that is not pertinent and that may be offensive to the admissions committee.

Students with other uncommon characteristics, especially sexual preferences that may offend the admissions committee, are generally ill advised to make these facts known. Remember at all times that members of the admissions committee are also human beings with faults; even the most astute scientist can be less than objective at times.

A local interviewer, while convenient, may be more critical of you, may emphasize professional over academic achievement, and may represent a lost opportunity to impress the admissions committee directly.

If you are genuinely unable to travel to the school for an interview, you may be asked to interview near where you live. Many schools will ask alumni or other practicing professionals to conduct interviews. This may be to your benefit, but it can also be to your disadvantage.

Unfortunately, you will have little say in who interviews

you. The school will select the local representative based on who lives near you and who is capable of conducting a rigorous interview. Those selected are frequently insightful individuals, meaning "critical" from your perspective. They are already in the field of practice, or they may be faculty members in other schools. Both situations present certain hazards.

People in practice will usually be active and devoted members of their profession. Having gone through years of training and now slaving away in the trenches, they may be especially critical of aspiring new entrants to the field. Are you willing to work as hard as they did? Are you willing to make the required sacrifices? Will you fit into the "brotherhood"? Would they like to work with you or have you work for them? These are the types of questions they will be asking themselves. These may not be the questions that the school has asked them to ask you. Still, the answers to these types of questions will likely be communicated to the admissions committee. This could be good or bad for you. And even if you are not asked these questions directly, you may need to address them anyway.

The practitioner interviewer will often look for professionalism, maturity, interpersonal skills, and communications ability.

Practitioners may also be more pragmatic than academics. Their questions may test you, almost as if you were working for them. They may be less interested in your pure academic brainpower than in your interpersonal skills, your ability to handle yourself on your feet, or your ability to communicate. If you are relatively young (or tend to appear that way), or if you have more brains than composure, you may be better off with an interview by an academic faculty member. If you appear polished and professional, communicate well, and seem to fit into a variety of professional situations, you may be better off with practitioners.

Local faculty interviewers may not use the same standards as the school to which you are applying.

If you are asked to interview with a faculty member from a local school, you may face other hazards. Often these people will have friends on the faculty at the school to which you have applied. They also may be rivals as well as friends or colleagues. They may tend to evaluate you in terms of their school's own academic and professional standards, which may be tougher than those of the school to which you are applying.

Academic faculty at another institution may not be as friendly or as sympathetic to you as you might desire. Remember, they are interviewing you as a favor to another faculty and may not be excited about taking time to talk to you. Practitioners, for that matter, may also feel this way, but they are generally more likely to be helpful, since they often feel either obligated or honored to be asked to help out.

Interviewers are human beings with emotions, feelings, and biases.

Regardless of where you are interviewed, there are some principles to keep in mind. Remember, above all, that you are dealing with an individual human being who is susceptible to a variety of emotions and feelings. As noted in other chapters of this book, every contact that you have with a school can be critical. Even students with very high board scores and excellent grades are sometimes rejected; avoid feeling overconfident, and always work to ensure your acceptance.

You will usually be contacted by the school to schedule the interview. There are relatively few situations where all applicants are interviewed. If the school has numerous applicants for a few slots, they may not want to interview everyone. If the school has few applicants for the available positions, there may be little point in interviewing, since most students will be accepted anyway. And, as noted previously, some programs do not interview because it takes too much faculty time, is viewed as introducing biases, and does not contribute information that is needed for decision making.

An interview is often a sign that you are a serious contender for admission or that there are important items in your credentials that the school wants to clarify.

If you are interviewed, it usually means that you fall into one of two categories. In many professional programs all applications are initially screened, and those meeting certain minimum academic standards, primarily involving test scores and grades, are selected for interviews. In this instance selection for interview is indicative of having passed the first hurdle. To determine if this is the situation you face, you can ask the admissions secretary if all applicants are interviewed. The answer should tell you where you stand going into the interview.

The second category of interviewing involves borderline candidates who present some special question or problem. Sometimes outstanding applicants are accepted without interviews, and only marginal candidates may be interviewed to determine if their personal attributes will push the decision one way or the other.

An interview may be requested because the faculty has a question about the applicant's credentials. This is not necessarily bad. For example, the committee may be impressed with your credentials but may feel that their program could be the wrong one for meeting your career objectives. Of course, an interview in this situation can also put you in jeopardy, since the committee may not be as impressed after the interview as they were before, or they may be left with the wrong impression about your career goals; the interview could raise more questions than it settles.

You may want to request an interview if you feel that you can sell yourself to the admissions committee; but this can be risky.

Although the program usually requests an interview, the applicant may also do so. Requesting an interview can be a wise strategy in some situations. Remember that interviews are a burden on the faculty, who may resent the extra time they must spend with you. However, if you are enjoyable enough to talk to, you might counteract this.

An unsolicited interview can benefit the marginal applicant. An otherwise outstanding applicant is probably taking some risks interviewing when it is not required. The marginal applicant, however, may have little to lose and much to gain. Such individuals might have borderline grades, relatively poor test scores, or a lack of experience. If you feel you might be such an applicant, you might want to contact the program and ask them what the range of grades or test scores of accepted applicants was in the preceding year; most schools will give out this information so that you can roughly judge where you stand in the competition. If you fall far from the range of accepted applicants, you clearly are at high risk. In some instances, such as medical schools, where academic criteria are generally applied to all applicants without much leeway, those with low scores have little chance for admission no matter what they do. In some of these situations you may not even be able to request an interview. However, if there is some flexibility on the part of the program in the extent to which "paper" credentials determine the admissions decision, you may be able to improve your chances through a personal appearance.

If you request an interview, try to meet with a member of the admissions committee and to make a strong positive impression.

Thus, if things look bleak from a purely academic viewpoint, and if you are confident that you can make a strong personal impression, you probably have little to lose by seeking an interview. Request a formal interview. If you are only to get an informal interview, be sure that you are meeting with a member of the admissions committee or, at the very least, someone who will be sure to communicate the results of the interview directly to the committee. An interview granted with a staff person, counselor, admissions secretary, or interested faculty member who has no contact with the committee may only be a palliative that will do you little good.

Your purpose, if you fall into the last-ditch category, is basically the same as that of anyone being interviewed except that you must make an especially strong positive impression. Above all, you must attempt to justify your relatively dismal prior academic record or experience history. You must show enthusiasm for the degree program and your willingness to work hard. Above all, you must provide the rationale for the admissions decision to be positive in spite of paper credentials that may not alone justify acceptance.

An interview is a complex and critical element in the admissions process.

Regardless of how the interview is arranged, it is a critical stage in the admissions process. An otherwise strong applicant can be rejected based only on thirty minutes of poor performance in an interview. Years of careful academic preparation, outstanding credentials, and hard work can be offset in just a few minutes. No matter how confident you are, always keep in mind that you are on trial, that you have not yet been accepted.

Your interview will usually be scheduled by the admissions secretary. It is wise, as noted previously, to treat this individual nicely. A casual remark by a staff member to a faculty member about how discourteous you were on the phone can create a very bad start for the interview. While it is unlikely that there will be any permanent damage from your early contact with an admissions secretary, why take any chances?

Schedule the interview when you are likely to give your best performance.

You should set up the interview, if you have a choice, at the time of the day and even the day of the week when you usually function at your best. Some people are morning people, while others perform better in the afternoon. Decide when you put on your best performance and try to schedule your interview accordingly. If you usually perform better in the middle of the week or on a Friday, use this information to your advantage. Unfortunately, you will not be able to select the time that's best for the people doing the interviewing, and while you may be doing well, they may not!

Prepare in advance for the interview.

Once the interview is scheduled, you should begin to prepare. First and foremost you must carefully and completely read the written material published by the program. You should thoroughly understand the program and its academic requirements.

You should compile a list of solid questions to ask at the interview and think through in advance answers to questions you are likely to be asked.

You should develop a list of questions that you want answered in the interview. This will show your depth of understanding of the program and impress the interviewer with

The Interview and How to Handle It

your probing and thoughtful questions. Your list should not be so long, however, as to imply that you have questions about every detail and that you cannot figure some things out yourself. Your list should not have many questions that relate to admissions processes, however, since this information is available from the brochure or catalog or from the admissions secretary. The faculty members interviewing you, or their delegates, generally will not want to discuss such matters for very long.

The second preparation you should undertake, well before the interview, is to think through carefully the types of questions that you may be asked. You should have answers already formulated in your mind to the more significant questions, especially those that relate to your career goals, to problems in your prior record, and to your reasons for choosing the field and particular program.

Since one purpose of the interview is to determine how well you have thought through your personal goals and academic and professional interests, failure to have proper answers to these types of questions can be a serious problem. Take some time and carefully think through how you would react to probing questions about your interests, aspirations, and personal philosophy. You would be well advised to write out answers to such questions ahead of time.

If you are fanatical about these matters, you might also want to have a friend, preferably someone who has gone through interviews before, interview you in a mock setting, to test your acumen as well as to work with you in identifying your weaknesses in communicating. While few applicants go this far, such preparation may be quite beneficial.

In advance of the interview explore the field of practice you seek to enter.

The third way in which you can prepare for the interview is to investigate in advance the field you are seeking to enter.

Again, remember that the admissions committee is also accepting you into the field of practice and will be very interested in the degree to which you have an understanding of that field, especially in the context of your personal goals. You can strengthen your hand by reading about the field and by going out and talking to professionals. This last suggestion is probably the most important. In most fields the best way to find out about the real world is to talk with practitioners. They can tell you a lot about the field you think you are interested in. You can ask them any question without harming your chances of admission. You can try to decide if this is the field in which you really want to spend the rest of your life. They can tell what the training is like, too.

Indeed, you are best off talking with practitioners before you even apply for admission. Many people choose training programs based on what their parents want them to do, on exposure to the field through the media, or on other relatively flimsy evidence. The reality of the job may be substantially different from what you think it is. You are best served by having a realistic knowledge of the field and its opportunities and shortcomings.

Having prepared adequately for the interview, you might want to relax for a few days preceding your performance. Then, just before the interview you should get a good night's sleep so that you look healthy and rested. You will want to appear only slightly nervous and moderately but not overly confident.

Dress conservatively for the interview and make a good first impression.

In dressing for the interview you should keep in mind that the admissions committee is selecting people to enter the field of practice. Given two otherwise equally prepared applicants, the one that looks the most professional may be the one admitted.

While it may not seem so to you, casual dress conveys disrespect for the field and for the interview process. Your first impression is dependent in part on your physical appearance. You should make a pleasant impression, one that conveys professional competence. After you are admitted, you can return to wearing blue jeans and running shoes.

A male applicant should generally wear a shirt and tie, suit or sports coat and slacks. A clean and uncluttered appearance is probably best. There is no way to predict what the person interviewing you will think about different forms of dress. Thus, some conservatism will probably err on the safe side. Overdressing is also to be avoided. You do not want to look wealthier than the faculty member interviewing you! Avoid flashy clothes and accessories.

The female applicant should also follow a relatively conservative approach. A suit or conservative dress is probably best. Since you may be interviewed by either a male or female faculty member or both, you only want your clothing to convey professionalism. Avoid expensive or elaborate accessories and jewelry. Slacks can also be worn but may be a negative factor, depending on the interviewer.

Of course, in some instances, such as art school, you may want to appear more casual to reflect a creative, nonconforming personality. Obviously, common sense is important in deciding on what image to present through your appearance.

Arrive on time and relaxed for the interview, and always be friendly and courteous.

The first impression you make will help set the tone for the interview. Above all, be on time. While you may be kept waiting before the interview, you should arrive in ample time. It might even be wise to arrive early enough to allow a few minutes to relax before the interview. If the travel was tiring or left you a little winded, you will want to restore your appearance and composure before the interview. Perhaps freshen up, and then take a short walk down a hallway for a few minutes before reporting for the interview. You will have been told where and when to report. Allow adequate time to park your car or to walk from the bus stop or taxi stand. Also allow adequate time to find the appropriate offices. You will impress no one by explaining how you got lost.

Watch what you say and to whom, and follow established interview procedures.

You will probably first check in with a secretary or admissions officer. You should be extremely courteous to these individuals and be careful about any remarks you make. Assume that any students in the hallway are in the program, and do not make any rude or disparaging comments of any sort.

When you check in, you will be told the exact procedures for the interviews. These vary widely. In some instances you may be interviewed by a number of faculty and students at one time. In others you may be asked to interview with only one person or with a faculty member and a student separately. Exactly who interviews you and in what order and format is entirely up to the program. However, you can obtain this information in advance by asking the admissions secretary when calling to schedule or confirm your appointment. If you are being interviewed by practitioners or alumni or faculty from another program, you should also request information as to the format for these interviews, what positions the interviewers hold, and how much time the interview will require.

Be respectful to everyone you meet; be open and honest, but also exercise caution in what you reveal.

Everyone who talks to you is important. If you are interviewed by students, you should assume that they are on the admissions committee or that their comments will be passed on to the committee. While some programs allow you to talk to students on a more or less informal basis as a way of providing you with additional information, you can rarely be sure as to what information about you will find its way back to the admissions committee. Therefore, it is best to be on your best behavior regardless of whom you are talking to. Also, while the students may be friendly and frank with you, you should be relatively formal, pleasant, and not overly frank with them. Be especially wary of revealing any inner uncertainties or insecurities you have.

Your most important interviews will be with faculty members or the admissions officers. In some instances you will be interviewed by a staff member whose job is to conduct interviews; this individual will have full authority to act for the program and may be more skilled at interviewing than are faculty members.

Your initial contact with the person conducting the interinterview is important. You should be friendly and warm. Do not be overly aggressive, but be conservatively confident of yourself. Begin by shaking hands and saying hello. Some brief small talk, perhaps commenting on the beauty of the campus, is a nice opener. However, the interviewer does not want to waste a lot of time on small talk.

Most likely the interviewer will lead the discussion. Some people believe that they can retain control over this type of situation by trying to take charge of the interview. The interviewer will probably not appreciate your adopting this strategy.

How you handle yourself in an interview can be almost as important as what you say.

You might allow the interviewer to initiate the conversation. Most interviewers will start with relatively "simple" questions such as asking you what your career interests are and how they developed. Your answers should appear natural and not prefabricated. You should appear to be frank and open, not coy or deceptive. The way in which you respond is almost as important as the response itself.

You should generally avoid raising any red herrings or substantial questions about yourself. Your objective in the interview is, at the least, to do no harm. If possible, you want to sell yourself and convince the admissions committee through the interviewer that you are competent and would be a good addition to the program and the profession.

You can expect to be asked about your understanding of the field, your personal and professional goals, and your experience and academic record.

Most of the questions you will be asked are raised because they are concerns that the interviewer has, either for you personally or for everyone who seeks to enter the program. You probably cannot expect to fit the bill ideally on each and every question; thus you should not try to tell interviewers solely what you think they want to hear.

In general you will want to appear interested and knowledgeable about the field you are seeking to enter; the absence of either characteristic may be a serious flaw. You should also seem like a nice, pleasant person. You should not be argumentative, but on occasion you may want to take issue with the interviewer. Some interviewers may even try to elicit a sharp retort.

Stories used to abound about applicants to medical schools being asked political questions related to United States involvment in Vietnam during the 1960s. While there is certainly a potential for abuse in the interview process, concern over such matters is probably exaggerated. Responsible political opinions can probably be expressed without severe consequences. More radical philosophies may be acceptable as an expression of personal insight or may be taken as an indication of naiveté and immaturity. Don't assume that all faculty members are of any particular political persuasion. Political opinions should sound like they represent a rationally constructed view of the world.

It is difficult to anticipate all of the questions that you could be asked in the interview. Some questions will probe your background; these include such general-information questions as why you chose your undergraduate major, what your undergraduate course of study included, how you selected elective courses, and what your educational and career goals were during your early college years. These questions should be answered relatively openly and honestly. Of course, responses that would indicate that you were not a serious student in college or that you randomly selected your course of study will not look good. In addition, you should appear to have had some forethought on the relationship between your undergraduate major and the graduate area you are now seeking to enter.

You will have an opportunity to explain areas that may concern the admissions committee.

A number of serious questions could be raised. You could, for example, be asked why you switched majors in college, especially if you switched a number of times. Great concern will be expressed in the admissions committee if it appears that you are uncertain about the course of study you are now seeking; the applicants with the most long-standing determination will likely be the ones accepted. You should be able to explain your change of majors without impinging on your potential professional or academic abilities. For example, you should not state that you switched out of a mathematics major in college because it was too difficult if you are now seeking to enter a field that requires quantitative competence.

Another obvious area for questioning is your undergraduate academic performance, the single most important aspect of the admissions requirements. This includes your college, major, coursework, and performance as measured by grades. You should be prepared to offer explanations of any course in which you received lower than a B or its equivalent. Any grades below a C will trigger concern almost automatically and must be explained adequately. Your explanations should reflect your special circumstances, if any, such as personal or family problems (which have been resolved and will not affect your graduate performance). If the subject in which you did poorly is not at all relevant to your proposed field of graduate study, you might claim that you are just not very good in that area. Think these things through before the interview.

Any course you failed may require an especially good explanation. A failure may almost automatically exclude you from acceptance. But remember that the committee knew your grades before inviting you to interview and therefore must see some merit in your overall record.

You may even be asked to explain good grades.

Any exceptionally good record may also require explanation, as surprising as that may seem. Remember that you are dealing with professional academics, who not only work in academia but who may have spent eight or ten years as students preparing to become faculty members. You cannot easily deceive them. If you have an exceptionally good academic record, you may simply have selected an easy major or taken easy courses. Some majors and some colleges are especially suspicious. The absence of science or math courses and the presence of well-known easy courses may mark you for investigation. You may have to do some fast talking, perhaps by asserting that you truly enjoyed these subjects and thus did well.

You will probably be asked a variety of questions about your background, interests, family, skills, and aptitudes.

You will also likely be asked a variety of peripheral questions to determine if you are a "good citizen." These include questions on extracurricular activities, summer employment, and so forth. This may be more important in professional than academic graduate programs. You may also be asked when you decided that this field would be your life's work and why; some interesting history would be useful. You might also reflect on your prior exposure to the field, what excited you about this career opportunity, and the like.

You may be asked some questions about your family. This may be to probe your home life, to determine the environment in which you grew up, or simply to satisfy the curiosity of the interviewer. In some fields having family in the profession can help your chances of admission, although there is some debate over exactly how much that helps.

You will likely also be asked questions about your skills and aptitudes. Obviously not all of your abilities are reflected by your grades. The interviewer will be probing to determine your intellectual skills and achievement potential. The types of questions you may be asked are difficult to predict. You may even be asked knowledge-type questions about your undergraduate specialty, almost as if you were being quizzed. Don't freeze up; take a second or two and think through a solid answer. Even if your answer is somewhat incomplete or even partially wrong, you can score points if you present a systematic, logical response.

Throughout the interview you will be tested for analytical and conceptual abilities as well as for verbal skills. Every response, regardless of the topic area, will reflect your ability to communicate concepts.

Emphasize your academic and personal strengths; play down or justify your weaknesses.

You may be asked to discuss your personal strengths and weaknesses. You should emphasize your academic and professional abilities. Many strengths will already be apparent to the interviewer. Avoid emphasizing any major personal faults or inabilities. The best weaknesses are those that suggest enthusiasm and commitment such as working too hard, trying to do too much, or acting too fast in a situation because you want to succeed.

Some of your weaknesses may already be apparent to the interviewer, and so you many want to provide explanations. The interviewer has your academic record and your letters of reference; from the first moment of meeting you the interviewer has been analyzing your personality, communications ability, and personal habits. If you have weaknesses that are likely to have become apparent to the interviewer, you might try to explain some of them. Do not, however, go out of your way to raise new questions. Your explanations of weaknesses should reflect a very positive attitude that you can and will overcome any handicaps.

Be prepared to explain why you chose this field and this program.

Other questions that may be raised involve the field of practice you seek to enter. You might be asked what you think of the field, what its problems and shortcomings are, or what you personally can contribute.

You will probably be asked why you want to attend this particular school or program. You may be asked where you heard of the school or what its reputation is. These questions are designed to find out how informed you are about the program and how motivated you are to enter its hallowed halls. You should appear knowledgeable and interested; interviewers are likely to be more receptive to you if you seem to have a genuine interest in their program. On the other hand, you probably won't have to indicate that you have put all of your eggs into one basket. If you are really committed, you might be expected to apply to more than one school to increase your chances of admission into at least one.

While the questions you are asked can vary widely, their objectives are usually similar. These include determining your motivation, your knowledge of and interest in the field and the program to which you have applied, explanations about your background, and any unusual circumstances that are relevant—in the minds of the admissions committee, at least. Politics, personal habits, mannerisms, attitudes, and other topics you might feel are not relevant may still be included in the information that is collected through the interview. That is why the interview can be biased and potentially unfair. However, this is a battle that the applicant is not able to fight.

There are other purposes for an interview. The most important of these, as noted previously, is to provide you with information about the program and perhaps even to provide a public relations opportunity. Remember that there are only a limited number of highly capable applicants for whom many programs compete.

If you talk to current students in the program, ask the hard questions: How difficult is the program? What is it like to be a student here? How good is the faculty? How receptive to students are the faculty? What content areas do you learn? Do people get jobs when they graduate? Is there financial aid? Are there good times along with the work? Is there contact with the field of practice? Are the laboratories good? And so forth. As mentioned, your comments to the students may be fed back to the admissions committee; you should ask if your meeting with students will be off the record. Since many admissions committees include students, and students talk to each other, some caution is justified in any event. But there is immense value in talking to current students, and, after all, a major purpose of the admissions process is to ensure that you make the right decision.

The interview is a one-shot opportunity; use it wisely.

You cannot fully prepare for the interview. It is unlikely that anyone could anticipate all of the questions that might be asked. But you have only one opportunity to impress the admissions committee in person, and this is it. Poor performance in the interview can be devastating to even the most academically impressive candidate. Whether you feel this is fair or not is irrelevant.

The important points with regard to the interview are worth reviewing. Be confident but humble, and answer all of the questions as directly as is prudent. Remember that your physical appearance is also important. The same goes for your personality. Whether you think it is fair or not, admissions committees can justify rejecting any academically well-qualified applicant whom they feel would not fit into the profession.

The interview is far trickier than most applicants, and probably most admissions committees, realize. More subjective information is involved in the interview than possibly in any other aspect of the admissions process, with the possible exception of the letters of reference. If an interview is required, it is likely that the committee is seeking subjective information, since it already has considerable objective material. You are being examined under a microscope and under pressure.

The interview is an opportunity. If you can sell yourself to the admissions committee through the interviewer, you may overcome years of mediocre college performance, a lack of adequate experience, or any other flaws. It is also a time of risk, and every applicant would be well advised to remember that seemingly strong applicants do receive rejection letters.

The Interview and How to Handle It

The interview is probably the most controversial aspect of the admissions process—at least it should be viewed as such. The role it plays varies in importance, depending on the program. As an applicant, you will know little of such matters until it is too late. You should approach the interview with caution and preparation, with confidence and apprehension, and with respect.

PART III *Special Situations*

CHAPTER 11 *Using Connections and Back-Door Admissions*

FOR MANY YEARS there have been rumors that certain medical schools are very receptive to applicants whose families donated large sums of money. While these allegations have never been firmly proven, rumors and innuendoes about back-door admissions surface frequently. Sometimes students point an accusing finger at classmates, assuming that they used connections to help in the admissions process.

There is, in all likelihood, some truth to the assumption that some individuals have an advantage because of connections or other seemingly extraneous factors. The degree to which this occurs varies greatly, and the overall frequency is totally unknown. The extent to which any individual program is susceptible to such pressures is also unknown.

Attempts at using connections and other forms of back-door admissions are highly risky—but may be worthwhile considering.

Many applicants are well aware of the potential for using connections and back-door admissions; others may not be as aware as they should be. When to use such pressure tactics is also a topic for which little guidance can be given the applicant.

By and large the application of pressure on the admissions committee through connections is not kindly received. While one or two members of the admissions committee may be receptive, the other members may be offended. In addition, if the admissions committee includes student representatives, they are likely to be especially opposed to the acceptance of such an applicant. Therefore, the use of pressure must be considered to be an extremely delicate subject. After all, the committee may reject an applicant in response to undue pressure, and then the effort will have backfired.

Each individual must weigh the moral issues involved in using connections.

To many people the use of connections and other forms of back-door admissions may be morally wrong or otherwise offensive. To others this represents another approach to improving one's chances for admission just like any other additional item of information on the applicant's background. Some applicants excel in one area, some in another. The morality and fairness of using such added opportunities is, in the final analysis, up to each applicant. Friends, relatives, and others may offer advice, but you must live with the consequences and should think maturely about the advantages and risks involved.

There are many forms of influence that can be beneficial. Some of these may be justifiable, while others may be reprehensible. Your entire future may be dependent on the admissions decision, and so you may rationalize any tactic that facilitates admission.

The applicant with a fine record is likely to stand a good to excellent chance of admission regardless of whether or not outside pressures are brought to bear on the admissions committee. Such an applicant may be risking more than is likely to be achieved by the use of connections to further facilitate admission. On the other hand, as many well-qualified individuals can attest, there is never an absolute assurance of acceptance.

The applicant with a weak record may stand little chance of admission regardless of the degree to which pressure is exerted. In this instance the applicant may be better off considering other career alternatives. The individual in the middle, with acceptable but not outstanding credentials, is likely to benefit the most from any pressures that can be brought to bear on the admissions committee. But this individual may also be at higher risk of offending the committee.

Admissions committees are, generally speaking, composed of sensitive individuals who are fully aware of any attempts to pressure them on behalf of an applicant. Therefore, it is wise advice to think, and think again, about the extent to which such pressure will serve your best interests. In addition to the moral issue there are pragmatic concerns that must be thought out before acting.

There are numerous potential ways of exerting pressure on the admissions committee.

The avenues through which an applicant can put pressure on the admissions committee are numerous. Some are subtle, while others are overt. Many are available only to an elite few, while others are available to many applicants who are not even aware of the possibilities. The extent to which each avenue is open and the degree to which each should be used are dependent on an individual's personal situation, moral and philosophical approaches, and opportunities.

The most overt strategy, perhaps, is to buy one's way into a program or school with a very large donation, perhaps through the generosity of a parent. This opportunity is available to few applicants and is difficult to document. Those few applicants in a situation to pursue such an approach presumably do not need further advice on the topic. However, there are in fact many other less expensive and more available strategies that the typical applicant can consider using.

Pressure can be exerted on your behalf by influential people, especially faculty members.

The most common approach to using connections and back-door admissions probably is to have individuals who know the applicant exert pressure on his or her behalf. The individuals that can effectively do this include faculty members at the school to which the individual is applying, professional colleagues of faculty members at the school, alumni, friends of faculty or administrative officers, large donors, and other individuals with some sort of clout at the school. You may find that if you think through everyone you and your family know, there may indeed be someone who can exert some degree of pressure. Since minorities and the disadvantaged are less likely to have access to the power structure of society, back-door admissions are discriminatory.

Someone on the faculty or closely allied with the faculty, such as the dean or other administrative officer of the school, can be especially useful. A large donor can be very powerful. Most alumni are less likely to have significant influence.

The influence of a faculty member in the school or program that you are seeking to enter can be substantial. Unless the applicant has especially poor credentials, a faculty member may be able to ensure a positive admissions decision. Sometimes, of course, members of the admissions committee may disqualify themselves from the decision process. But even in this instance a few words of assurance about the potential of the applicant can be most beneficial.

If you personally know or are related to a faculty member of the program you seek to enter, you might want to discuss the extent to which he or she would support your application. They may be more uncomfortable than you might anticipate in applying pressure on your behalf. And keep in mind that the application of pressure on behalf of an applicant is rarely overt and direct; it is more often achieved indirectly through statements of support or perhaps offhand comments to other faculty.

There are other people at the school who can also apply pressure on your behalf. The deans and other administrative officers can express support for an individual, in writing or through verbal communication. The members of the admissions committee may feel under some pressure in these instances, especially since the administrative officers control budgets and personnel allocations. Junior faculty may also feel under some pressure to give special consideration to such applicants. Of course, such an approach may not endear the applicant to the faculty in the long run.

Alumni and donors can be somewhat useful to the applicant. A large donor can have undue influence in any school, and especially in private schools, since they are more dependent on endowments than are public schools. The susceptibility of any program to such pressures is difficult, if not impossible, to determine.

Program alumni can be very helpful in attesting to your potential contributions.

Alumni of the school and especially of the specific program can also be helpful to the applicant. Alumni often like to think of themselves as having strong bonds of loyalty with their programs. However, this bond is more of a one-way street than most schools will admit. It is relatively rare that, at the graduate level, alumni can exert enough pressure to substantially affect the admissions decision. Of course, an alumnus who is also a large contributor to the school falls into the donor category, in which case the story may be different.

Yet there are ways alumni can be very helpful to the applicant. Practitioners in the field can speak to both the applicant's potential as a student and as a contributor to the field of practice. A letter of reference from an alumnus who knows the applicant as a friend or relative is generally less impressive than one where the relationship is that of coworker or supervisor. But an alumnus can be very specific in support of the applicant by relating personal qualities, potential for academic achievement, and the like to program goals and priorities, and such connections are worth considering.

Alumni should be relatively open about their relationship with the applicant. Any communication, then, whether it be in the form of a letter or a telephone call, can be rather laudatory. It should address the exemplary character of the applicant, the strong interest in the field that the applicant has exhibited, and the fine mind and tremendous potential of the candidate. The alumnus should be enthusiastic about the applicant's potential to contribute to the field and to be a conscientious student. There is little room for exaggeration regarding academic abilities, since the admissions committee has considerable documentation of that. Indeed, misrepresentation or inappropriate exaggeration along these lines will be easily discernible and therefore could discredit the entire effort.

Practitioners can help support your application by noting your professional potential.

Other individuals may also be useful in exerting pressure on the admissions committee. Practitioners in the field, especially those with an affiliation to the program, may be valuable contacts. This is particularly true for professional programs that use practitioners to lecture in the classroom, to take students for field work, and so forth. These practitioners, if they are friends or relatives of the applicant, are an important connection. They can be effective in communicating on your behalf with the program director or a friendly faculty member. Bending admissions might be viewed as an unspoken quid pro quo for the time the practitioner spent on behalf of the program.

Using Connections and Back-Door Admissions 135

Letters from people such as politicians tend to offend the admissions committee, although they may sometimes help.

In addition to the more common types of pressure, there are less direct but sometimes more effective methods. For instance, pressure can be exerted by politicians, especially in governmentally supported universities. While these approaches may not always seem like direct pressure, in almost all instances the admissions committee is likely to consider letters of reference and telephone calls from politicians to be pressure tactics, which can potentially backfire.

As discussed in the chapter on references, letters and telephone calls from politicians are often not well received, although on occasion such a strategy may be startlingly successful. The admissions committee will be skeptical that the politician personally knows the applicant well enough to provide a valid and objective assessment. There is also a feeling of outright pressure that is hard for many faculty members to swallow. Of course, if the politician actually knows the applicant well—for instance, if the applicant worked for the politician—there is no reason that a personalized letter should not be submitted.

Connections can help you in a number of ways, including providing an entree that might otherwise not exist.

While it is generally very difficult to use connections to gain an acceptance that otherwise would not have been forthcoming, connections can open other doors. The use of connections can gain you an entry into the admissions process and thus increase the extent to which you are seriously considered; and, if the applicant has some potential competence, connections can get the applicant's foot in the door.

Some people can apply sufficient pressure on the admissions committee to gain the applicant an interview. This may be a major opportunity that allows applicants a chance to sell themselves in person. A faculty member, a professional colleague, or an alumnus can be helpful to this strategy. Your connection might also be able to encourage the admissions committee to give more serious consideration to an application. Thus, someone who would have been rather routinely rejected might be given more careful examination, and thus may have an added chance for admission. Obviously, there is no substitute for strong credentials, and the use of these strategies is often only marginally beneficial.

Even having a current student in the program speak out on your behalf can be potentially helpful.

A few other remote opportunities for using connections also are worthy of mention. Personally knowing a current student in the program may offer some opportunity for enhancing one's chances for admission. Many applicants fail to realize the potential value of having a student who is currently in the program speak out in their behalf. If there is an opportunity, the student can note your abilities. If the admissions committee is undecided, a very positive boost from a current student, while no substitute for strong credentials, may help.

A student wishing to express support for you can do so either by talking to a member of the admissions committee, especially one who is personally known to the student, or by writing a letter to the committee. If there are students on the admissions committee, the information can be passed along through those channels also.

If you have worked for a nationally recognized faculty member at another university, that person may be able to exert pressure on the admissions committee through a telephone call or in writing. The connection should imply that the applicant is unusually outstanding and that their professional relationship has lead to the conviction that the applicant is worthy of all possible consideration. This can be an effective approach in drawing attention to the applicant. An outstanding candidate can especially benefit from the strong support of a nationally known person, but such an individual may have little difficulty gaining admission anyway.

There are a variety of creative back-door strategies that can be considered.

There are other approaches to back-door admissions besides using connections. One of the most common is to apply to another degree program within the same university, then attempt to transfer into the desired program after one or two terms. This is risky when transfer students have to go through the same admissions processes as any other applicant. In addition, the faculty may remember you as someone who was previously rejected, and they may still be apprehensive. Such a roundabout strategy may work eventually, but it is risky in terms of the time expended and the questionable chances of success. Some guidance from faculty or admissions counselors may be helpful.

A worthwhile strategy may be to apply for a less popular concentration area.

Many applicants are unaware that in some programs specification of a tract, concentration, or major field of study can have a substantial effect on the admissions decision. In some areas of emphasis the program may receive relatively few applications. It may be possible, through careful questioning of faculty, staff, or students, to determine the most advantageous areas of concentration and thus increase one's chances of acceptance. In most programs, although not necessarily all, it is relatively easy to change areas of emphasis after matriculation.

There are probably a few other avenues for back-door admissions that have been attempted over the years. In point of fact there are very real limitations to these strategies, and even some degree of risk. However, there are some strings that may be worth pulling, and an applicant with the need or opportunity to do so should certainly at least consider the possibilities. The final decision requires careful thought before acting.

CHAPTER 12 *Women and Minorities*

THERE IS LITTLE DOUBT that over the years women and minorities have been underrepresented in professional schools and, probably to a lesser extent, in graduate degree programs. There are a number of reasons for this situation for women. They have often been typecast into roles that preclude professional careers. In addition, women have faced professional and cultural discrimination. And admissions criteria were probably stricter and more subjective for women applicants in the past.

Along with women, minorities have faced professional discrimination and difficulties gaining admission to training programs.

Minorities have also faced significant barriers in education, especially in such fields as medicine and law. Lack of access to educational and cultural opportunities that result in good credentials and rapid career development have almost automatically excluded many capable minority candidates from admission to graduate and professional programs. A lack of financial resources has placed a severe hardship on many members of minority groups who otherwise have considerable talent and promise for advanced study. Traditionally white-dominated fields have tended to exclude minorities. There are many unfortunate circumstances that have led to the underrepresentation of both women and minorities in professional fields.

Today's world is very different in regard to the admission of minorities and women to advanced training programs. There has been increasing recognition of the inequitable tradition of discrimination in admissions over the years. Pragmatically, there is now considerable social pressure to alleviate the underrepresentation of these groups in professional fields. As gatekeeper of many professions, admissions committees must come to grips with the need to admit more women and minorities to virtually every field of practice.

There are now often advantages for minorities, and sometimes women, through preferential treatment.

As a result of the pressures that are felt by admissions committees, there are now some additional opportunities that both women and minorities can take advantage of in seeking admission to graduate and professional programs. These opportunities are generally more available to minority group members, especially those who are black, Spanish, or American Indian, than they are to women. And in some circumstances, especially where the school has a religious affiliation, even religion may be a factor in an applicant's favor.

As in other aspects of the admissions process, you need to weigh the advantages and disadvantages of emphasizing your sex or race. Philosophically, you may feel that it is inappropriate to "trade" on your race or sex. Of course, you probably won't be able to hide your sex from the admissions committee. The more difficult issues are associated with race.

Although you must consider your own situation, some words are in order that can help you decide whether to "use" race to your advantage. When a personal interview is required, your race will probably become known to the admissions com-

Women and Minorities

mittee. In the past this was sometimes how the admissions committee would exclude minorities. Today, by and large, the opposite situation exists.

Remember that most admissions committees are actively seeking qualified minority candidates. By making known your racial affiliation you can assist the admissions committee in this mission. Regardless of whether the motivation of the schools is to redress past inequities or to respond to societal pressures, admissions committees in most fields are seeking what are termed "qualified" minority applicants. Thus, all minority applicants would be well advised to make their status known. This does not, however, ensure acceptance.

Over the past few years there has been a tightening up of admissions standards for minorities, although there are still expanded opportunities in most fields.

The recruitment of minorities nationally has taken a number of turns over the past twenty years. Initially, of course, there were very few minorities in most graduate and professional programs. Then, largely in the late 1960s and 1970s, there were big pushes to increase minority enrollments. These efforts included a multitude of initiatives, ranging from lower traditional admissions standards to special programs at the high school and college levels to prepare minorities for advanced training. Many minority applicants who were successfully recruited into programs experienced difficulty later in completing some of their academic requirements. Unfortunately, in recent years there has been a backlash against the admission of people who do not appear to be fully qualified academically. As a result admission standards for minorities have been increased in the last couple of years in some fields. In addition, there has been an unfortunate easing of social pressure on schools to improve minority representation in professional fields. This, too, has led to less vigorous efforts in minority admissions. On the other hand, there is still a national commitment to expand opportunities for minorities, and there are vastly greater training alternatives for minorities today than throughout most of the nation's history. Furthermore, there is now a much larger pool of potential minority candidates for graduate and professional-degree programs.

The result of these trends is some increased difficulty of admission for minority applicants in some programs as compared to a few years ago; but there are still many opportunities. Many, if not most, programs actively seek and welcome applications from minority applicants who are deemed "qualified." The primary concern about minority applicants at the present time is the interpretation of the term "qualified."

There is severe competition among schools for the best minority students, although minimum standards have increased in recent years.

The term "qualified," when applied to minority applicants, has traditionally implied standards and criteria that are somewhat lower than those required for other applicants but that still hold the promise of academic success. Many minority applicants to graduate and professional programs these days are, aside from the issue of academic credentials, highly committed and personally qualified. Indeed, the level of commitment is often higher among minority applicants, many of whom have traveled much harder roads to success than the average middle-class white student.

There is still a shortage of "qualified" minority applicants applying to many schools. Therefore, there is competition among schools for the best applicants. As a result, many minority applicants can call their own tune, bargaining for financial aid and the like. The most outstanding applicants, assuming they have the appropriate undergraduate education, can practically select any advanced training program in the United States.

The minority applicant who is not top of the line but who is creditable can also choose from a variety of programs. Obviously, as the quality of qualifications declines, the applicant's opportunities also are reduced.

It is usually difficult to determine how far academic standards will be lowered for minority applicants, if at all.

The point at which a minority applicant would be considered less than "qualified" is obviously important, but it cannot be easily determined. Most programs do not want to admit that they reduce some of their academic requirements for minority applicants, and most programs are vague on how far they do lower admission standards, if at all. Since there is a lot more to a candidate than grades and test scores, there is little reason for being secretive; minorities can offer a lot more than nonminorities in many ways, both to the program and to the field of practice.

Generally, a minority applicant whose grades are a bit below the mean for all entering students, and whose test scores are even comparatively a bit lower than that, would have a fair chance of admission in many programs. You might even ask the programs to provide the mean grade and test score data for minority and nonminority applicants. However, it is wise to ask what the program includes in the minority category. Asian students, for example, tend to have relatively high grades and test scores, frequently not having experienced the same degree of academic deprivation as many other minorities. Foreign students should also not be included in the computations, since they can substantially skew the data. Ideally, you should ask for the data for your own minority group—if there are enough such students in the program to provide meaningful data. You should also, when possible, seek personal interviews with counselors or other representatives of the programs to add to your insight.

Grades are probably more important than test scores for most minority applicants.

A minority applicant with good grades but poor test scores or good test scores and relatively poor grades is obviously better off than an applicant with poor performance on both measures. However, it is sometimes unclear whether poor test scores or poor grades hurts the minority applicant more, especially if the other measure is respectable. Standardized tests have never been a strong point for minority applicants, especially those from disadvantaged backgrounds. Admissions committees know that test scores may be extremely misleading for these applicants. However, very low scores will inevitably raise the issue of whether the applicant has the requisite academic abilities, all things considered, to get through the program. Since there are minimum academic performance criteria that the student must meet to graduate, most programs are increasingly apprehensive about accepting anyone who seems doomed to failure. The applicant is not very well served by being accepted either, if he or she is likely to flunk out. The availability of special tutoring and other assistance programs for students may be considered, but these programs have been reduced in recent years as a result of the severe financial pressures now faced by higher education.

The minority applicant with relatively low grades but high test scores also represents a risk. The high test scores would be well received, of course, but the low grades at the undergraduate level would raise the issue of whether the applicant could successfully compete at the graduate level. Since there are many undergraduate schools that are as rigorous as many graduate programs, the applicant's school and major field will also be of importance in judging performance.

The well-qualified minority applicant should have little difficulty in gaining admission, while marginal applicants will face a harder time than they would have a few years ago.

The bottom line for minority applicants, then, is fuzzy. Generally there are somewhat lower expectations in terms of grades and test scores in many, but not all, programs. Times are changing, leading to more rigorous admission standards for minorities compared to a few years ago. Poor undergraduate performance and low test scores are a severe handicap that the minority applicant may not be able to overcome regardless of his or her own attributes. But if there are some indications of a person's potential academic success, combined with personal qualities that appeal to the admissions committee, the minority applicant may be able to gain acceptance. As noted, the highly qualified minority applicant with good academic credentials should have little trouble gaining acceptance to most graduate or professional programs.

The messages and hints contained in this book are very important to minority applicants. Presenting the best possible picture, doing so in a professinal manner, and appearing interested and committed to the program and to the field of practice are all as important for the minority applicant as for anyone else. Seeking advice and investigating the options available before applying are also important for every applicant.

Who is considered a minority will depend on the program, but usually blacks, Spanish-surnamed people, and American Indians are included.

Finally, and perhaps most confusing of all, is defining what constitutes a minority applicant. Generally, but not always, admissions priority is assigned to blacks, certain Spanish-surnamed individuals, Puerto Ricans, and American Indians.

By and large, foreign students, regardless of race, are not considered in the same manner as United States minority applicants. Some Asians, Pacific islanders, and others may also be considered minority applicants in certain situations. Black schools may or may not give admissions preference to white applicants. Some individuals may gain from dual preferences, especially minority women. Veterans may enjoy some preference under certain circumstances, especially minority veterans. The handicapped may entertain some preference, again especially if they are minority group members, although they may face other obstacles as discussed elsewhere in this book. There are obviously many possibilities, and the best source of information is the programs to which you are applying.

Women generally are no longer as discriminated against as in the past, but they must meet the same standards as men.

The situation for women, alas, is not quite as promising as for minorities, unless the woman is also a member of a minority group. Over the years women, too, have faced discrimination and have had difficulty entering training programs, especially in professional fields. But in recent years the number of women in these programs has skyrocketed, especially in such fields as business administration, medicine, and health care. In some areas women are even "overrepresented" now in student numbers as compared to the general population, while in others, including medicine, the increase in the numbers of female students has been substantial, though not equal to the percentage of women in the population.

The bottom line for women is that there is far less discrimination, if any exists at all, in admissions but that women by and large must meet the same admissions requirements as men. In other words, while there are always exceptions, women's credentials must be as strong as those required for male applicants. There are also probably a few fields, one of which is rumored to be veterinary medicine, in which women may need slightly better credentials than men. But the data suggest that overall, excluding minorities, admissions standards are comparable for both men and women. Fields that have relatively few women, such as engineering, may be actively seeking female applicants, although admissions standards are likely to be rigorous.

While there are fewer female students in many programs than the prevalence of females in the population would suggest is equitable, the number of female applicants is often also lower. The proportion of applicants accepted as well as the quantitative data on those admitted in fields such as medicine suggest that admissions standards are similar for both males and females. Of course, standards could be lowered for females in this situation in order to increase the number of females in these schools, but this does not appear to be a favored approach.

It will be many years, if ever, before true "equity" is reached in most professional fields.

The number of minority or female acceptances into training programs does not significantly address the issue of misrepresentation in the field of practice in the short run. Since the number of new graduates each year in any field is usually small compared to the total number of practitioners, it would take many, many years to reach a point where there is an equitable number of women and minorities working in the field of practice. As the number of older, predominantly white males who graduated in the past decreases, and as the number of minority and female graduates increases, the proportion of nonwhites and nonmales in many fields will slowly increase. But this process takes many years. And if the proportion of females or minorities accepted remains lower than the "equitable" population percentage, as is likely in many fields, there will never be true equity.

Female applicants should also be aware of potential stereotyping and male chauvinism. While there are pressures to avoid this, admissions people are human beings, with all of the frailties that entails. There is simply no way to completely rinse society of these tendencies. Thus, you need to be especially cautious in interviews and in writing narrative statements to ensure that you protect a professional image.

Women who have been out of the work and school environment while raising families face further hazards. The difficulty of returning to a rigorous educational program, especially if combined with family responsibilities, should not be underestimated. If a divorce and single parenthood is also involved, the pressures could be tremendous. In addition, admissions committees may view the older woman as having a significant gap in time and experience, compared with someone who was working outside the home. Financial aid may be less available to the woman who is dependent on a husband, whether she wants to be or not. Women returning to the work force need access to education that can improve their job prospects. Women with less desirable jobs who want to upgrade themselves also need to be able to obtain more education, especially in professional programs. But they also face some significant problems, and it is important to recognize these added barriers where they exist.

Women and minorities now face a vastly different world with greater opportunities and fewer obstacles. Not all doors are open yet, and not all obstacles have been removed, especially for minority groups. All applicants have a duty to themselves to maximize their chances of success in life, and the admissions process is one area where change has been dramatic and relatively rapid.

CHAPTER 13 *The Decisions, and How to Cope*

THE END RESULT of all your efforts to gain admission to graduate or professional school will be a letter telling you the good or bad news. The letters you receive will largely determine the future direction that your career assumes, at least initially. The schools' decisions and your next actions are obviously very important to a lot of people. And, if the decisions on your applications are negative, knowing what recourse you have is of vital concern.

You will be notified of the admissions decisions by mail or telephone, the telephone call sometimes being used for especially desirable applicants.

The decision that is reached by the admissions committee can be communicated to you through the mail or, less often, by a telephone call. The telephone call often is an indication that you are especially attractive to the school. However, the program may call if they know from prior communication with you that you are especially anxious to hear from them, or if there is relatively little time available before the school or program needs a response from you. Often, however, it is a compliment for a school to notify an applicant by telephone of the admissions decision.

Be sure each program admissions office has your current address and telephone number at all times, including your work telephone number, if any.

Remarkably, applicants sometimes fail to hear from the schools they applied to as soon as they might like for a very simple reason: Some applicants move and fail to notify the school of their new address and telephone number. It should go without saying that all applicants who are serious about a program should endeavor to keep the program informed at all times concerning their current address and telephone number. Inability to contact you readily may hinder the functioning of the admissions committee. You may lose valuable time in replying to an admissions offer if the program has difficulty in contacting you. In the final analysis, while it is unlikely, you may lose more than time if the program is unable to communicate readily with you. For example, the program may need clarification on a point in your file prior to making a decision; a delay may occur in processing your application if the information cannot be obtained, as discussed in chapter 4. Enough said about this issue.

If you receive a positive response from the admissions committee, you have cause for celebration. A period of enjoyment and self-assurance can be your reward for all of the trials and tribulations of the admissions process. If you receive more than one positive response, you will have to make some hard choices. And even if you are accepted into only one program, this is a good time to ponder your future once again.

There are some practical issues and concerns that you need to think about with regard to the admissions decision and your response. Of course, a period of excessive festivity and fun is justified, and should this discussion appear too rational and cautious at such a joyous time, you can be excused for another round of celebration. But sooner or later, serious time must be set aside for careful consideration of your acceptances.

The letter of acceptance contains information on the terms of your admission, and it should be read very carefully.

First, the letter of acceptance should be carefully reviewed. While one should reread the praise that it inevitably contains, there is more to consider. The letter of acceptance is also often used to convey certain information to an applicant. This material generally falls into two categories: "mandatory" and informational. The first category should be of more concern.

The letter of admission is part of the "contract" between you and the program. As such, it is used to convey information that the program wants to state in a forceful and, in a sense, legal manner. This information usually centers around the terms of your admission.

Often a program will accept an applicant on specific conditions or terms. Some of these tend to be more explicitly spelled out than others. In most universities a student is protected by certain safeguards. Any mandatory constraints on your acceptance must be outlined in the official letter of acceptance. It would be unfair to admit students and then, when they show up, tell them that they are expected to meet certain additional requirements that other students do not have to meet.

In other words, the letter of acceptance will specify any unusual circumstances that apply to your acceptance. The letter can tell you a lot about how you were perceived by the admissions committee and where you stand.

Regardless of the content of the acceptance letter, you will be required to meet all program requirements, which are usually stated in the catalog, brochure, or handbook.

The absence of a statement regarding special requirements in the acceptance letter, of course, does not mean that you are excused from requirements that apply across the board. For example, in graduate school, students are usually required to maintain a minimum grade-point average. Every student may be required to meet prerequisite course requirements, which are spelled out in the catalog. Thus, you must read the catalog because you will be held to all requirements regardless of the content of your acceptance letter.

Generally speaking, the catalog or similar document constitutes a contract between you and the school for a specified educational program. The school agrees to provide specific training, while the student agrees to maintain a minimum grade-point average and to complete any required courses. Any exceptions that pertain to an individual student must be documented and based on established procedures. For example, if you do not meet the minimum grade-point average or course requirements, you may be dropped from the program.

Any nonstandard phrases in your letter of acceptance are very important and must be carefully reviewed.

Unconditional letters of acceptance are the norm. Any deviation from the norm suggests potential problems with your credentials, the most common of which relate to academic performance.

Questionable academic preparation or performance is addressed in a number of ways. Many programs, especially in professional schools, will require that you complete additional coursework prior to matriculation. This may be because of poor performance in courses you completed at an undergraduate level or because of an absence of courses that would substantially help you handle graduate-level work. While you may initially be offended by this type of conditional acceptance, it is usually to your advantage to complete the suggested coursework. Faculty members have considerable experience with the educational needs of students and are only trying to prepare you to handle the material covered in the program.

Sometimes additional coursework may be suggested but not required. Again, the advice is given to improve your preparation and should be followed when feasible. While students these days sometimes don't want to admit it, the faculty do possess a certain degree of wisdom in these matters.

Although you would be wise to follow the requirements of the admissions letter, you may be able to avoid them.

Although it is sensible to follow the program's requirements that you complete certain courses prior to matriculation, there are some loopholes that you may want to take advantage of. First, you may be able to demonstrate that the required courses are not available in your area. Second, you may be able to convince the program that returning to school to complete additional coursework would create a financial hardship. Finally, you may be able to arrange with the school to complete the courses as part of the first semester of the program. However, this may extend the time required for completion of the degree. If you really want to take a risk, you might even ignore the stipulations of your acceptance letter and show up at the appropriate time, pleading for acceptance. Of course, this strategy is not especially to your benefit and certainly will not impress the faculty.

Conditional acceptances that reflect questions about your academic abilities should prompt you to examine your motivation and aptitudes before plunging ahead.

Your letter of acceptance may reflect other apprehensions about your qualifications. Your acceptance may be conditional on the successful completion of one or more terms in the program with some minimum grade-point average. Conditional acceptances of this type obviously put you at some degree of risk; you may want to discuss your potential for meeting these added requirements with the faculty. However, you will probably find that grading in graduate and professional schools is not all that stringent, and admissions committees are usually shrewd enough that most conditionally accepted students eventually graduate.

Occasionally an applicant may be accepted subject to the submission of additional credentials. These may include standardized test scores, transcripts from courses currently in progress, or additional letters of reference. Students who are currently enrolled in undergraduate programs are usually accepted contingent on evidence that the undergraduate degree has been awarded. This usually must be accomplished prior to matriculation and generally requires the submission of a final transcript after graduation.

The program can require you to pass through any number of additional hoops before matriculation, including taking courses, working, or submitting additional credentials.

There are still other contingencies that you may find in your letter of acceptance. Some of these may be only suggestions, while others may be requirements that you can ignore only by risking the loss of your place in the class. These mandatory contingencies may relate to further work experience, especially in professional programs. You may be required to continue working or to seek an acceptable position so as to gain further experience prior to matriculation.

Another common requirement in letters of acceptance is that the student attain competence in fields related to the new program. For example, you may be encouraged to learn algebra or calculus prior to matriculation. Again, these requirements are not meant to be penalties, but to improve your ability to function successfully in the classroom.

The Decisions, and How to Cope

Many individuals accepted for advanced study lack adequate communication skills. Some faculty think this applies to most students. Rather than attempt to teach the fundamentals of writing and public speaking to graduate students, the program may suggest or require that you complete "remedial" courses in these areas prior to matriculation. This commonsense advice may be difficult to swallow, but it is worth heeding.

You have a right to a clear understanding of any contingencies and the reason they were imposed.

There are many other possible contingencies that may be contained in your letter of acceptance. These may or may not seem fair to you. You should always have a right to know what is meant by each requirement. If any requirement is vague or unclear, you should feel free to contact the program for further information. You may even want to request an explanation or justification for the contingency.

Once accepted, you will gain a new status with the program. Every accepted applicant, regardless of contingencies, has been anointed. You have become a member of the club—or at least have been asked to join. Rather than dealing with you as one person among perhaps hundreds or even thousands of applicants, the program is now dealing with you as one of the select few incoming students. You are now someone who is welcome at the school. As a result, you now have a much greater ability to elicit information from the program, and this ability should be used as you make your decision about which program, if any, to enter.

If you are especially lucky, you will have letters of acceptance from more than one program and will be in the enviable position of having to decide from among a number of alternatives. However, even if you are accepted to only one program, you must make a "go/no-go" decision.

If you are accepted into a program, you still may not want to enter it.

If you are offered a place by only one program, you may not want to accept it. If the school is your first choice and you are positive of your decision to seek advanced training, then there is no real issue, and you can readily reply. But if you are accepted by your second or third choice, or worse, you need to invest considerable thought before taking action.

Usually someone's first choice is the one that they feel most comfortable about. Many people have their hearts set on attending a specific school. Not gaining acceptance to that school, regardless of the number of other acceptances, can be a real disappointment. This can be unfortunate, especially if you did get into another school with a solid national reputation.

A long shot is to ask for reconsideration of your application if you are rejected; another option is to reapply the next year.

If you don't get into your first-choice school but have other acceptances, you need to analyze your options. If you are seeking training in a highly competitive field such as medicine, you may be well advised to think twice before passing up any acceptances. In a less competitive field, however, you may have other alternatives. One alternative is to contact your first-choice school and inform them of the situation and of your desire to attend their program. Ask for a reconsideration of your credentials. (This is discussed further, and in more detail, in the next chapter.) Another alternative is to pass up your acceptances and reapply the following year to your first choice. Many people would consider this somewhat foolish and risky. But if the first-choice school has a better educational program and a national reputation, this may not in fact be such an extravagant action.

Once you have been accepted, you must judge which program is best for you.

If you are fortunate enough to gain admission to more than one school, you need to weigh the advantages and disadvantages of each. The first step in this process is to consider all of the schools for which an acceptance is in hand. Read the acceptances and determine which, if any, are conditional. Are you willing to meet these conditions? If not, these schools can be excluded from further consideration.

Each school among the remaining possibilities should be assessed in terms of its national reputation and your personal career objectives. In addition, the costs of each program should be examined. Any offers of financial assistance should be taken into account, as is discussed in chapters 15 and 16.

In evaluating the schools that have accepted you, it is your turn to be judge and jury. You want to look at the programs and schools as critically as they looked at you. Your ability to perceive the differences between the programs will be very important.

You may want each program to submit information to you. This may, at first glance, appear to be a bit of retribution for all that it put you through as an applicant. However, you have a right to know what you are getting into and to request any information that helps you make this very critical decision. At the least you should have a detailed brochure about the program, including required coursework and elective options. The credentials of the program, including a listing of the current faculty, should be available. The prior success of the program in education is important, especially some history of how long the program has been in operation and of how successful graduates of the program have been in obtaining employment and in climbing the ladder of success. You may want to check the program's references by calling faculty at other schools or your advisers from college to get their opinions. Above all, remember that you are making a crucial personal decision that you will have to live with for a very long time.

Once you assemble information on each program, you must compare their attributes and liabilities. You will also want to compare the characteristics of each program with your own personal objectives and career goals.

Be absolutely certain of your decision, and then contact all of the programs that accepted you.

When you reach a final decision, set it aside without taking any action for a few days. Then review all of the information you collected, and rethink your decision to ensure, as a double-check, that you are totally comfortable with your choice.

Once your decision is final, communicate with each program that sent you a letter of acceptance. Those that you have decided not to attend should be so notified. Often there will be a waiting list of applicants who might be accepted if positions in the entering class become available. Your letter to the program may open the door for another applicant. In addition, it is simply common courtesy to inform the programs that accepted you of your final decision. If you like, you might want to tell them which program you decided to attend. They will be interested to know which competing program they lost you to and why. It might even help them improve their program.

Start out on the right foot by graciously communicating with your new program.

Obviously, you must also communicate with the program you have decided to attend. Tell the admissions staff that you will indeed be attending so that a position can be reserved for you. Provide the program with an accurate mailing address, valid until you report for registration, so that they can keep you informed of items of interest that come up from time to time. You may also want to apply for financial aid, ask for housing assistance, or clarify any prerequisites or conditions for admission.

Your letter accepting the offer of admission should be nicely written. It may be retained in your permanent student file and will be a constant reminder to the faculty of how pleasant or unpleasant you were at the start. It is also a chance to thank the admissions committee for expressing their confidence in you. You may also want to praise the admissions office staff and secretaries, who probably worked harder on your behalf than you are aware. They will appreciate your praise, and it might give you a good image prior to registration. In the same vein you will want to conscientiously complete all required forms that the program sends you after acceptance and prior to matriculation. Remember, you are always being judged by the faculty, and you will need their help when you graduate.

You may want to defer your admission for a year or two; many programs will agree to this if you have a legitimate reason for doing so.

Sometimes it is wise for applicants to ask for an admissions deferral. A deferral, if properly executed, can ensure you a place in next year's class. Deferral can be useful for a number of reasons. If you have a severe illness, for example, you may want to wait a year before you start graduate study. Frequently applicants want to work for another year or two before starting school to gain more work experience or to earn money to help pay for school. Some people simply do not feel mentally ready to start graduate or professional studies when they are supposed to report.

A deferral can usually be easily handled, and many programs are receptive to such a request if you have a good reason. A written request for deferral should be sent to the program. A preliminary telephone conversation may be used to determine the program's policies toward deferrals.

Your written request should be very gracious and should express flattery at being accepted. It should then provide the detailed reasons why a deferral would be beneficial to you. If possible, you should demonstrate that you will be better prepared for advanced study by virtue of waiting. For example, further work experience or additional coursework will contribute to your being a better student.

Most programs will grant a deferral, but in some places, especially in public universities, an outright deferral may not be possible. You may be assured that since you were accepted once, you are highly likely to be accepted again. However, anything short of an actual deferral with assured reacceptance, in writing, does not constitute an absolute guarantee. In addition, any equivocal statements should be a source of concern. If you must reapply and again compete for a position, you run a risk of being rejected the second time. You should be cautious if an absolute deferral with assured acceptance is not forthcoming in writing.

Such are the difficult but satisfying decisions that face the successful applicant. Not everyone falls into this category, and the next chapter addresses some alternatives for those facing rejection. In the final analysis success in a reputable graduate or professional program is only the beginning of a long career, and most of that career will be determined by the steps that lie ahead rather than the one just completed. But it should be reassuring to know you have stepped successfully through a veritable minefield and have now opened the all-important admissions door to the hallowed halls of some university so that you can eventually practice your chosen profession.

CHAPTER 14 *What to Do If You're Rejected*

FOR ALL THE HOPES and enthusiasm of many applicants, the time of truth may not lead to a positive outcome. A series of rejection letters can be extremely demoralizing to one's ego. But this is also a time for you to develop new strategies and approaches.

Many applicants want to enter very competitive fields for which training opportunities are limited. Some people are unsuited for advanced study, while others, although qualified, cannot be accommodated in the number of entering spaces available. Wise applicants will have followed the advice contained in the previous chapters and should, at the least, have maximized their chances of admission.

If you are rejected by all of the schools to which you applied, you should rethink your goals and strategies.

Failure to gain acceptance at the first try is neither a personal insult nor necessarily evidence of inability to succeed in one's chosen field. Rather, rejection letters should be viewed as a new challenge, a call to arms requiring further hard work and deep thought. There are other avenues that can be followed.

If you are rejected, especially if you are rejected by a number of programs in the same field, you must begin a frank assessment of your aptitudes and career choices. This is not to demean your abilities, but rather to point out that everyone has their areas of strength and of weakness, and being frank about these is necessary for a realistic appraisal of where you can now consider going educationally.

Rejection by many programs in the same field can indicate a number of possible problems. The most obvious of these is that you simply fail to meet the minimum admission requirements for programs of study in your chosen field. In most instances this failure is due to academic deficiencies, but other shortcomings, such as inadequate work experience, can also be a factor.

There are some quantitative ways you can determine if your credentials are outside of the realistic parameters for admission, at least in terms of academic abilities. The best approach may be to contact each of the programs and ask for the mean or median grades and standardized test scores and the range of values for all of the people admitted to the class, as suggested earlier. If your credentials fall substantially out of the range or are not consistent with the mean, you were probably rejected for academic reasons. If your credentials are consistent with the scores of those accepted, it is likely that you were rejected for other reasons, such as inadequate work experience or poor recommendations. Thus you might also ask the programs what the average number of years of work experience was of those accepted as well as other relevant information.

You simply may not be a viable candidate for the type of program you want to enter.

A realistic appraisal of your credentials is essential. Frankly, some people who apply for graduate study simply do not have the academic ability or drive to be good candidates. You must take stock of your strengths and weaknesses. If you are simply not suited for graduate study, perhaps you would be better off thinking about other alternatives.

Rejection letters may also indicate that you have inadequate credentials to compete for admission in your chosen field. You may want to consider entering a related but less rigorous field of study. There are many alternatives available to people today, and you must realistically assess where you best fit in.

Sometimes well-qualified applicants are rejected simply because there are too few places in the entering class to accommodate everyone.

Rejections may also be indicative of factors that are not necessarily solely related to your academic credentials. Many applicants are rejected because of limitations on the number of positions available in the entering class. Although it may sound like a cliché used in rejection letters, many professional and graduate programs receive more applications from qualified applicants than they have room to accommodate. You may want to consider reapplying in a future year. This points up the need to submit an application that maximizes your chances for admission no matter how qualified you may feel you are.

There is another area in which reapplication is likely to be advantageous. Some applicants, for a variety of reasons, only apply to one program. Doing so severely restricts the chances of admission. It is very unwise to put all your eggs into one basket, but there are times when you have to do so. You may not be in a position to relocate, you may feel that only one program in the country is good enough for you, or you may have to seek admission to a particular school for financial reasons. Sometimes applicants are sponsored by their employer on the condition that they attend a specified school; this situation should be brought to the attention of the program.

Persistence through reapplication can pay off in an eventual acceptance.

If you are rejected because of lack of space and are otherwise qualified, you should stand a good chance of admission on reapplication. If you want to pursue this, request an interview with a member of the faculty to discuss your application and to obtain a realistic assessment of your situation. While it is unlikely that any firm commitment can be obtained, you can note on your application that the meeting occurred and that you were given strong encouragement to reapply.

If you were rejected for relatively legitimate reasons, upon reapplication you are likely to face the same barriers as the first time around. In addition, most programs compare a reapplicant to the current pool of applications. Thus, if the applicant pool in a subsequent year becomes more competitive, you would be even less likely to be admitted. Of course, if the number of good applications falls off, your chances of admission would increase.

If you are going to apply again next year, take advantage of the available time to strength your application.

If you intend to reapply, you will have time to address any deficiencies that exist in your credentials. Use this time wisely. Contact the programs and ask what you can do to improve your chances of admission. This may lead to suggestions that you seek additional work experience, take further coursework, or retake the standardized tests required for admission. This is extremely valuable advice.

When you gain the advice of the program on how to strengthen your application, you also potentially have a foot in the door. The application, when resubmitted, should emphasize that you took this advice and did what you were told would be necessary to gain admission. You will thus have

What to Do If You're Rejected

demonstrated your commitment, and this may weigh heavily in your favor when the application is reviewed for admission the second time around.

If you are rejected, you may still have some options.

Of course, not all applicants want to wait to reapply. There are some other options. One of these is the waiting list. Many programs place on a waiting list applicants who are qualified but for whom there is inadequate space. If accepted applicants turn the program down, spaces in the entering class will be allocated to those on this waiting list. If you are placed on a waiting list, let the program know that you are still very interested in attending and ask if there is anything that you can do to become a high-priority member of the waiting-list pool. Again, it rarely hurts to show interest and commitment.

A rejection, if you are relatively well qualified, may also be subject to appeal. While this is a long-shot approach, it may be worth an attempt. The admissions committee is, by and large, obstinate. They have to be able to deal with everyone who is rejected. However, a qualified applicant who is rejected may have some standing to appeal. An obviously unqualified applicant, of course, would be advised not to pursue an appeal and to attend another program or consider other alternatives.

An appeal is not actually an appeal, since there is really no higher decision-making authority than the admissions committee. Rather, the appeal is really a request for reconsideration. You should approach the admissions committee through the admissions secretary or other designated official. If possible, and if necessary to gain action, an approach through a faculty member may be advisable. You should reiterate in polite, rational, and strong language that this is the program that you very much want to attend. Specific legitimate reasons for selecting this program should be stated. You should request, in some cases almost insist, that the admissions committee re-review your file.

Don't take a rejection personally—rethink your strategies and start over again.

A rejection should not be taken personally, as difficult as it is to accept. It is a signal that something is wrong. Many rejected applicants will feel that there is something wrong with the admissions committee or the program, but the program usually does not share this viewpoint.

Rejection presents, however painfully, an opportunity to take stock of your life. Perhaps advanced study is not the right step for you at this time. Perhaps you applied to the wrong programs. Perhaps you studied too little in college. Regardless of the personal impact, you must attempt to understand where things went wrong.

Not everyone will be accepted by graduate or professional schools. In large measure admissions decisions are based on a record that is accumulated during many years of college, and possibly many more years of work experience. While there are things that you can do to improve your chances of admission, there is little you can do to overcome a notably unimpressive undergraduate record, or the lack of adequate work experience, or the absence of good solid references—at least in the short run. This book can help you overcome some handicaps, but you must be willing to invest the necessary time and energy.

If nothing works after all of your efforts, even your persistence may not be enough. A very realistic appraisal of yourself is in order. However painful that may be, in the long run it may lead to a much happier life. After all, there is often more than one way to achieve a personal goal. Advice from teachers, friends, and relatives as well as professionals in related fields may also be helpful. Rejection can lead to a painful time in your life. But it can also lead to a valuable period of reassessment and reawakening. As always, it is up to you to make the most of the situation and to look out for your own best interests.

PART IV *Financing Your Education*

CHAPTER 15 *Financing Your Education: Practical Considerations*

MONEY HAS ALWAYS BEEN IMPORTANT to graduate and professional students. But in recent years increasing educational costs and decreasing sources of financing for students have significantly heightened nearly everyone's interest in the money side of higher education. More and more, decisions regarding career paths and which programs and schools to attend, are being influenced by financial considerations. Therefore, it is very important to understand the factors that relate to financing your education as well as the alternatives still available to you. As emphasized throughout this book, doing your homework in all aspects of admissions, career selection, and choosing a program will pay off, sometimes even in dollars. Financing an education must be part of the process of seeking admission to schools. It will require your conscientious efforts if you are to have a successful educational experience.

Thinking about financing your education is very important and is increasingly difficult to do, but there are still many opportunities and alternatives available to you.

Surprisingly, there are many alternatives, even in tight times, for financing your education. You must recognize that there is a lot more involved than just the mechanical processes of finding out about sources of financial aid.

Perhaps the best place for you to start thinking about the financial aspects of your education is to find out what these costs actually are. As discussed in an earlier chapter, these costs include more than just paying for tuition and living expenses while you are a student. Computing these costs can lead to a better understanding of what you really want out of your graduate or professional education and, perhaps more importantly, what sacrifices you are willing to make. These costs must be weighed against the benefits that are likely to accrue to you in terms of career opportunities, financial rewards, prestige, and a lifetime of enjoyable work.

There are many substantial costs involved in obtaining an education, and they may extend far beyond the most measurable ones, such as tuition and living expenses.

The costs of an education, as mentioned earlier, are substantial. Even a one-year training program will require you to make significant sacrifices. As a result you need to understand and, if you decide to plunge ahead, be willing to accept these costs.

There are both direct and indirect costs involved in seeking additional education. The direct financial costs include tuition, student fees, room, board, other living expenses, transportation, books and supplies, telephone, instructional equipment or other special needs, and incidentals including entertainment for the few opportunities you will have to escape from the rigors of your studies.

Financing Your Education: Practical Considerations

Costs vary greatly from place to place and school to school; the quality of the education provided may not be directly correlated with the costs you are asked to pay.

Since costs for education, including living expenses, differ substantially among various schools and localities, it is imperative that you investigate these costs for all of the schools that you are considering. Tuition alone can vary from little or nothing in some public schools to in excess of $12,000 per year in some private medical schools. The relationship between tuition and other costs and the quality of the education that you receive may be very fuzzy. Don't take tuition or living costs as indicators of the value of the program.

State-supported schools usually have lower tuition and fees than private universities, but you must be a state resident to qualify for the lower fees.

The most notable characteristic of schools with lower fees is that they usually are state-sponsored institutions, while the higher costs are usually associated with private institutions or with public institutions charging higher fees for nonresident students. Among the most important decisions you will have to make, both financially and in terms of admissions, is whether to apply to public or private universities or to both types.

In the past few years many states have moved to raise tuition and fees, especially for out-of-state students, and in some instances these increases have been astronomical. Many states have passed legislation that requires nonstate residents to pay approximately the actual costs that the state incurs in providing them with an education. And in some states these increases have been tantamount to saying that out-of-state students are not welcome, that the educational system is designed, paid, and operated for state residents only.

There are a few ways in which you may be able to gain in-state tuition, and they can pay off even if you have to wait a term or two.

It is often relatively easy to change from out-of-state to state resident tuition status by declaring or establishing residency. This would have the effect of substantially reducing tuition bills for the remainder of your education. In most states, if you work full-time for at least one year (the time varies by state), you can easily declare resident status and thus immediately become eligible for state resident tuition and fees. There is a risk in doing this since you may not be accepted into the program you want at a school in that state. On the other hand, a somewhat extreme, but actually not unrealistic, option is to apply for admission to an out-of-state school that is especially attractive; then, if you are accepted, request that your admission be deferred for a year, find a suitable job, and work in the state during that interim year. By the time you start school you will be a state resident and will pay the lower tuition. The problem with this approach is that in some fields, such as medicine and dentistry, it is very difficult to gain admission as an out-of-state student (this ploy is one of the reasons the schools make it difficult). Also, find out if preference is given to state residents during the admissions process.

The conditions under which you can do this vary by state; some states have strict rules to safeguard against out-of-state students changing residency solely for the purpose of reducing their tuition payments. The universities to which you are applying can provide you with the specific rules and criteria that apply in your situation. Reading these rules carefully can save you thousands of dollars.

Private schools may cost more, but they may also offer a better-quality education and may have more sources of financial aid and part-time employment available.

Most private schools are on a pay-as-you-go basis, with much of the costs of education coming from tuition and fees. These schools, however prestigious they may be, have little alternative but to charge relatively high tuition, since they are not as heavily subsidized by public funds as are state universities. However, the better-known universities often receive federal and state grants and contracts for research and training, have endowment income, and can otherwise partially offset the costs of education through nontuition sources of funds.

Tuition and fees can be increased a lot, on short notice, and often; check out forthcoming fee increases and the possibilities of budget cutbacks that might hurt the quality of your education.

Tuition and fees can usually be determined from the catalog, but be warned that these costs are usually increased each year, and the increases can be substantial. Some universities may guarantee tuition for a period of time, but this is not common. Furthermore, you may not be told very far in advance of the forthcoming increases. Over two or three years many students in graduate and professional programs have experienced increases in these costs that they never dreamed possible. You should at least find out what next year's tuition and fees will be and what have been the recent annual percentage increases. Unfortunately, in many universities even the program directors do not have advance knowledge of the tuition for the next year, and in some state institutions the tuition and fees are not even set by the campus administration. The financial plight of many of the nation's states in recent years, and the ravaging effects of inflation, have played havoc with any attempts to plan for rational, and modest, annual increases in tuition and fees.

In some universities the quality of education has been eroding at the same time as tuition has been increased. This last point should encourage you to try to find out the status of funding support for the programs in which you are interested. Have there been any cutbacks that may have adversely affected the quality of the program? Are any planned? Cutbacks can lead to fewer faculty, larger classes, fewer teaching assistants, poorer laboratories and computer facilities, and lower faculty morale. On the other hand, many universities are eliminating programs so that the quality of the remaining programs can be maintained. Just be sure that your future program isn't on the hit list. There's nothing more depressing than being a student in a program that will be phased out. And it's nearly impossible to get references later in your career when your program no longer exists.

Living costs are difficult to determine, but you would be well advised to estimate them as realistically as possible so that you are not faced with high expenses that you did not plan for.

Living expenses can be determined from a variety of sources. While tuition and fees are established and published—although they can and do change each year, sometimes on short notice—living expenses are highly variable. They can differ markedly from the figures that are frequently provided in catalogs or brochures. This information may be outdated, is usually based on the "average" student (whoever that is), and may not take into account the quality of life that you desire. These published figures can only be used as a crude guideline, and they may have little applicability to your specific situation. What's more, these standard estimates may completely ignore such aspects of your life as growing children, medical costs, an expensive car, or expensive tastes in vacations. Even the estimates of the cost of books may not have much relationship to actual costs in your program. They may be based on estimates for all graduate or professional students, they may use old data despite the rapid escalation of book costs, or they may be so rough as to be useless.

The cost of housing can be very high, especially in college towns and urban areas, but there are ways to save money on your living expenses.

These are expensive times in which to live. Low-cost student housing, such as dormitories, is often not available to graduate students. Off-campus housing can be very expensive, especially in urban areas or college towns where the competition for space has driven prices up. If you are married, you may have substantially higher costs as a result of having to provide for your spouse and children. If your spouse works, he or she may not earn enough to offset the loss of your income and the other direct costs of education, such as tuition and books. In some areas the costs of housing and the availability of livable space are so restrictive that you will have to commute, thus increasing your transportation costs.

Plan in advance for unusual costs such as transportation, but remember that some sacrifices may be worthwhile for a good education that can advance your career in the long run.

There are a few additional comments of relevance on this point. If you anticipate traveling back home more than once a year, you should consider the costs of transportation, and especially of air travel, in deciding what part of the country to go to for your education. These costs can be very substantial, although there are frequently discount airfares and other ways to reduce the costs of travel, such as sharing rides.

There may be more opportunities for financial aid, for employment during school, and for a better job upon graduation at a school that on the surface costs more. As for tuition, you will have to weigh all of the options, and not make your decision based on the superficial differences in costs between the schools you are considering applying to. As you can see, there are few simple factors involved in selecting a program and financing an education.

If you want accurate estimates of the costs of your education, you will have to do some homework; it may be worth the effort.

The best ways to estimate costs for an education require some work on your part. The more accurately you want to know the actual costs, the more work will be involved. Keep in mind that you are usually going to enter the program at least one year from the time you apply, and costs can increase a lot in that period of time; this is especially true of rents. And even worse, if your program spans two or more years, you should be prepared to pay the increased costs that are likely to occur in all categories of expenses over that period of time. In a professional or academic doctoral program, which can last three to six years or even longer, the increases in costs can be astronomical. You may even want to consider an accelerated program to graduate quicker; sometimes this is possible if you can study in the summers or obtain credit for undergraduate courses.

The costs of books and supplies can add up; but these are not, in the final analysis, your biggest and financially most threatening items.

The costs of books, equipment, supplies, typing and reproduction services, and the like are often difficult to anticipate. In professional programs such as medicine there are good estimates available from the schools themselves. In many instances there are unique individual needs, such as the type of calculator you purchase, for which there are no solid estimates available from others. In any event, the best source of this information is the catalog and, of course, talking to students in similar programs. The costs of books and of many other supplies have increased very rapidly because of inflation. Again, the students who are already in a program similar to the one you want to enter can tell you both the current costs and the likely increases over the next couple of years. In some instances you may be able to reduce these costs by buying used textbooks, although you probably will want your own copies of many books and will always want to be sure you are using the most current edition. And in the final analysis, these are usually not your biggest expense items anyway.

Living costs are especially difficult to estimate but many students are able to live on relatively little money by making a lot of sacrifices in their standard of living. Are you willing to do so?

Living costs, more than any other factor in the financing of your education, will be very difficult to anticipate fully. Many students have an almost uncanny ability to control their living costs. It's possible to share an apartment, to eat low-cost meals, and to walk or take public transportation. Entertainment and vacations may suffer while you are a student, and you may have to make other sacrifices, such as reducing the purchase of new clothes or visiting your relatives only once a year if they live far away. These trade-offs are an individual choice, and the degree to which you are willing to make such sacrifices and modify your living style is an important determinant in selecting your school and deciding on your financial arrangements. The important point to make in this regard is that there are both income and expenses involved in graduate and professional education, and you may be able to exert more control over the expenses than over the income. Balancing the two is difficult but necessary, and your willingness to accept some compromises can have an important effect on your educational and financial planning.

While you can often reduce living and tuition costs, sometimes by a great deal, it may pay off more in the long run to attend a better school, even if it costs more.

Reducing living expenses is also the only major way to control your educational budget. Some very important decisions must be made in this regard. For example, if you are able and willing to live at home for nominal rent, you can obviously significantly reduce the cost of your education. However, this requires that you attend a local university, if there is one with the program you want. You may have to work extra hard to gain admission to that program if your choices are restricted to this one option. Furthermore, you may want to weigh the value of incurring higher costs but attending a more prestigious university. Or, if you are only accepted at a university that is far from home, you will have to decide if the added costs of attending that school are worthwhile.

Trading off living expenses against tuition and fees may also be a consideration. There may be a prestigious but expensive university nearby, so that you can live at home and use your limited resources to pay for tuition. On the other hand, if you prefer to live away from home, you can attend a less expensive university, to offset at least in part your increased living costs. Again, there are many trade-offs that you must consider, and most of these will affect which schools you decide to apply to.

Financing Your Education: Practical Considerations

There are many indirect costs to an education, as mentioned earlier, and these must be weighed as carefully as the direct cost. Are you willing to make the necessary sacrifices?

In addition to the direct costs of education, there are many indirect and less visible costs that you must also consider. These may even be more important than the direct costs. The indirect costs include the mental trauma of educational programs, especially those that are very rigorous or of long duration. These "costs" were discussed in earlier chapters and have a very real bearing on the level of your commitment to continuing your education. You should not underestimate how difficult or potentially unpleasant your years as a graduate or professional student can be. Again, talking to students already in the programs you are interested in is probably the best way to estimate these costs. And knowing how well you tolerate pressure and hard work may be equally important. In many fields there are some programs that are harder and some that are easier than the others. The quality of the education you receive is often directly related to the rigor of the program and to how hard you have to work. Any educator will tell you that the harder you work, the more you will learn. So again, you must decide how committed you are to learning and to performing well.

There are other important indirect costs, some of which are more easily measured than the mental anguish involved in education. The most important of these is probably opportunity costs, which were discussed in an earlier chapter. Many people quit their jobs or reduce their working time in order to pursue their education. This leads to a number of significant sacrifices, both financial and nonfinancial. Obviously you will lose income; in fact, it is not uncommon for new graduates of professional or graduate programs to earn less initially upon graduation than they earned in the jobs they held prior to entering school.

If you leave your job or reduce your level of effort, you may lose seniority and chances for advancement; part-time and night programs may allow you to continue working, but their quality may be lower than full-time programs, thus reducing your long-term payoff.

By being out of the active, full-time working world you will also lose seniority and the advancement that comes from plugging away year after year. If all goes well, you will rapidly catch up after you graduate, but this is not a sure thing any longer. The changing work environment in the United States has been modifying many long-held notions about advancement and the value of education. If you are able to work full time and pursue your education through time-off or night programs, you may be able to advance on both fronts at once. However, you must be cautious that your degree program is not viewed as being watered down, which often happens in these situations.

Obviously there are many costs to an education, and they are far more complex than you might have thought initially. However, there are also many more ways of dealing with these costs than you may have thought, and these are the subject of the rest of this chapter.

In the most fundamental ways, your decisions about where to apply must consider the financial aspects of your education. There are many decisions that impinge on the costs of an education and that affect your choice of schools. For example, whether you live near your family's home, perhaps to take advantage of low or no rent, or attend school farther away will obviously significantly affect your decisions about where to apply. The choice of attending a private versus a public institution usually will involve significantly different costs because of the governmental subsidies of public schools. Whether to attend a day or evening program is a pretty basic decision. There are many such factors that may be important to you.

Financing Your Education: Practical Considerations

Think in terms of the long-term potential of your education—look for the greatest benefit to your total career, not just the lowest-cost education.

The financially strapped student will likely seek to minimize educational costs through attendance at a local, publicly supported school. However, there may be more possibilities for obtaining financial support from institutions that are farther away. And there are very important trade-offs that relate to the quality of the education you receive. It is not a foregone conclusion that the lowest-cost alternative will be best for you in the long term. Better training, better career opportunities, chances for earning your way through school, and other considerations may result in the more expensive school's being a much better choice in spite of the short-term financial implications. It may be worthwhile for you to do whatever is necessary to attend the better school even if some sacrifices are required. This is the type of decision that each applicant must think through very carefully. In the long run you will regret any shortsighted decisions.

Your spouse may be your best source of financial and moral support—but if you are moving to go to school, check out jobs and childcare, and the strength of your relationship, in advance.

For many students the major source of support in graduate and professional schools is their spouse. Some spouses, ironically, find that they are discarded after putting their mate through school. This possibility should give pause to all spouses who are in this position. Some couples have made satisfactory arrangements where they take turns putting each other through school. However you work things out in your relationship, your spouse is potentially your most important source of financial aid, to say nothing of moral support and comfort through the often trying and difficult years of study.

There are a number of conditions that have to be satisfied for the spouse to be a meaningful source of financial aid. First, he or she must either be financially self-sufficient, have a rich benefactor, or work. Second, there must be arrangements for childcare if there are children in your family. Working spouses may also be a factor in choosing which school to attend, since many spouses will have difficulty in relocating and finding as good a job as they have now. It is always wise to check out the job market in a new area that you are considering before your spouse quits a job to relocate. Jobs can often be more difficult to find in areas around universities, especially in college towns. And remember that, no matter how skilled you think your spouse is, there are often many qualified, technically trained people near universities. Thus, you will want to carefully consider whether or not to relocate, and your spouse should explore the local job market in the areas to which you might move before you make any rash decisions.

Childcare is usually available in university communities. But again, you should carefully investigate before making any decisions. There may be long waiting lists for childcare services, the quality of the services or their value orientations may not meet your expectations and desires, and the logistics of the homes or centers may not be consistent with your family's life-style, schedule, or travel and work patterns. Again, investigate before you act.

Your parents may be a solid source of financial aid—but you may want to declare your independence of them or just borrow funds.

For many, if not most, students a traditional source of financial support over the years has been their parents. Parents have invested many dollars in education, but increasing costs have put a crimp in this pattern in recent years. As a result, more and more parents are facing limitations in the extent to which they can provide support. This is especially true of larger families and of support for graduate or professional education, since the parent may already have sent their child through four or more years of college. But there is certainly nothing dishonorable about asking your parents for some support, and if they are in a position to help out, their support could be very important to you. Again, you must decide if the investment in more education will pay off to your entire family over the years. Sometimes a loan rather than an outright gift from your parents is one way in which you can ensure that their investment will be paid back.

The support of your parents is something you will need to negotiate with them, but the extent to which they will help out may also be a factor in your decision concerning which school to attend. And they may be willing to provide additional support if that tilts the scales toward attending an excellent school rather than a mediocre one. Finally, many schools require that you obtain some degree of parental support if you wish to qualify for other sources of financial aid, especially if your parents can afford to help.

One note of caution, however, with respect to your parents is important. Graduate and professional students are usually older than most college students. At some point, and this varies by state and by situation, individuals are considered to be independent of their parents. You may want to take advantage of this principle to declare your independence and thus absolve your parents of any financial obligation to provide further support. You may also feel that your parents have given you enough already and that you do not want to take anything further. Once again these are all decisions that affect the many trade-offs that you must think through as you decide which schools to apply to.

You should plan on contributing your own resources, if any, to your education; these include savings and earnings from part-time or vacation work.

Most programs and most sources of financial support, except for awards based solely on academic merit, will require you to contribute to your own education. This is probably not an unreasonable expectation. It means that you should plan to spend some or all of your savings on your education, and if there is time, you might try to build up your savings in anticipation of doing so. In addition, where possible, you will want to consider working during the years you are in school. But this is not as simple as it sounds.

The best time for a student to work is when school is not in session, usually in the summers. However, some programs require you to study year-round, or they may have specific activities, such as field placement or thesis preparation, scheduled for the summer months. This would obviously preclude your working full-time. In addition, there are some instances in which the summer will be needed to catch up with missed work or to take additional preparatory coursework. Your first priority should always be your education. This is a very important point: It would be shortsighted of you to put so much effort into earning your keep that you flunk out or don't learn very much. But the majority of students will have an opportunity to earn money in the summers or during other vacations, and these opportunities should probably be taken advantage of. How much you can earn will obviously depend on how marketable you are, what skills you possess, and how readily you can find a good job.

Financing Your Education: Practical Considerations

You may be able to earn a lot of money even while you are a student—but keep your priorities in the right place, and never sacrifice your educational performance.

Many graduate and professional students have the ability to earn a lot of money through the use of their accumulated skills. For example, many students can work in construction, which can pay very well. However, you should carefully consider another trade-off—to work in an area related to the field you are now training to enter, rather than a potentially more lucrative but professionally less relevant occupation. Gaining experience in your chosen field, even at a low level of prestige and pay, can give you additional and valuable credentials prior to graduation and may also give you an edge in job placement or other postgraduate activities. Furthermore, by slaving away in the trenches you will demonstrate your commitment to the field to future employers. And last, but certainly not least, there is often a very valuable payoff in gaining experience that you can then relate to your classroom learning. This touch of the "real" world can make many lectures more relevant and help you understand the practical applications of the academic content of the training program.

You can make money by freelancing and by trading on your technical skills and willingness to do menial work, and at the same time gain valuable career experience.

In addition to working during vacations, many graduate students have considerable potential for participating in lucrative freelance work. There is nothing to stop you from freelancing while you are a student; of course, but unless you have extensive experience, you will not command high fees and the most exciting assignments. There are many jobs that a graduate or professional student can do very well and for which people are willing to pay. The faculty of your program may be able to assist you, acting in a sense as a broker, without fee, by putting you in touch with potential employers. And if you are in a technical field, your ability to perform nitty-gritty work, such as computer programming or assisting in a laboratory, can be highly marketable. Just be realistic about what you can competently do, and ask for reasonable but not excessive compensation. Also be sure to perform on time and as directed. The better you do, the more business is likely to come your way. Some graduate and professional students have done very well by freelancing while in school.

The university you attend may offer valuable employment opportunities that can also contribute to your professional growth.

Another important source of employment for students is the university itself. There are many opportunities in this area, although the possibilities are narrowing somewhat as the financial condition of many universities has suffered from inflation and decreased funding over the past few years. The most important sources of employment within the university for a graduate or professional student are student teaching or assisting in research. The pay can be very reasonable, and the work load can range from very light to very heavy.

An important factor in considering these jobs is whether you can benefit more from a teaching or research job. If you are eventually going to seek a teaching position in a university, some teaching experience is very valuable; you will learn a little about how to teach, something that most professors have little or no training in, and you will be able to add teaching experience to your résumé. If, on the other hand, you have little interest in teaching as a career, additional research work or other practical experience with a faculty member can be invaluable. In addition to the pay benefits, you will learn under the wings of a faculty member. This may even help you in completing your degree, especially if you have to do a thesis, and will also give you practical experience in starting your career. You may even be able to develop a thesis project out of a research assistantship. If you are in an applied professional field, you may want to work in a professional setting such as a clinic, an accounting office, or the like, depending on your field. Again, the more experience and commitment you can show throughout your training, the better.

You should not plan on working more than your studies will allow, and usually you can plan on more work time after the first term or semester.

There is considerable controversy among faculty members over how much graduate and professional students should be encouraged to work outside the classroom. In general the rigorous, demanding programs are likely to require the major commitment of your time, especially at the outset. Most students, except perhaps the very best prepared, should expect to devote most of their time to their studies, at least in the first year, and most faculty would offer this advice.

If you are attending a part-time program, including those in the evening or on weekends, you can expect to be exhausted most of the time. In addition, your efforts on the job may suffer from the drain of going to school at the same time you are trying to hold down a full-time position. If the program is really rigorous, the demands from both school and work will be substantial.

In many full-time programs your ability to assume some outside employment should increase after the first term or year of study. And in many graduate programs there is considerable time available to work after you are a little further along. Thus you might be able to plan for more working time as you progress in your course of study. Either program faculty or students currently in the program generally can provide you with accurate guidance on this point. Check this out in advance so that you can plan the financing of your education in light of the time that is likely to be available for working. Remember, though, that all students differ in their aptitudes, ability to use their time efficiently, and needs for study time. You will need to think through how you handle work and study situations, and whether you will indeed be able to commit yourself to both activities.

By waiting a while to start looking for part-time work, you may gain some advantage, especially if you impress the faculty and they are able to find you professional and financially rewarding employment.

The available work opportunities often become both more profitable and more relevant to your professional development after you have been in the program for a while. As discussed above, the ideal jobs for students are often those that have some component of professional growth. These include consulting, teaching or assisting in research, or working in the field. Often, if you wait one or two terms, while you study and do well academically, you will impress the faculty and have doors opened for you leading to part-time employment. In any event making a good initial impression will always be important, since it will set the stage for how the faculty views you throughout your educational program. The more positively you are viewed, the more the faculty will work for you in terms of job placement, references, and other educational and work-related opportunities. Again, there are important trade-offs that should always be thought through carefully. And these obviously require some hard thinking early on if you are to plan your educational career in terms of both gaining admission and financing your education.

Financing Your Education: Practical Considerations

You need to consider carefully all of the financial and admissions issues discussed in this book before deciding which programs to apply to.

Finally, you may be a very attractive candidate, and some schools, perhaps even the more expensive ones, may entice you with offers of financial aid. Additionally, at some schools you may be eligible for financial aid, grants, and scholarships that are unavailable at others. The real out-of-pocket costs of your education, after subtracting financial aid from your anticipated total expenses, are what you should really try to compute. And your computations should extend over the entire period of time that your education will require. These bottom-line figures should be considered in light of the quality and attractiveness of each of the programs you are considering. And, last but certainly not least, these factors must then be weighed against the difficulty of admissions and your chances of getting in, using all of the hints and tips contained in this book and your own best efforts. After you have thought through all of these issues and factors, made all of your trade-offs, and reached your decisions about where to apply, you will have done a very comprehensive job of looking out for your own best interests. You may also be exhausted and feel that you deserve a doctorate in higher education or accounting.

CHAPTER 16 *Financing Your Education: Sources of Funds*

THERE HAVE ALWAYS BEEN WAYS to finance an education. And over the years the rules of the game and types of aid have periodically changed. Your responsibility is to stay current with what is now available and to exploit those sources of funds for which you qualify. There are no shortcuts, and no one will do your homework for you. There will always be ways of legitimately getting money for your education, and you owe it to yourself to find out what they are and how much you can get.

> *Your first-line sources of financing your education are your own resources and your ability to contain living expenses and other costs.*

The most obvious sources of support for most students, as discussed in the previous chapter, are their own resources: family, savings, summer earnings, and the like. However, many students have available to them a wide array of other sources of support, and this chapter discusses many sources that may be open to you.

Of course, as emphasized in the previous chapter, there are many factors that influence the cost of an education, and in some instances costs may be more related to where you apply than to what financial aid is available. The costs of education include tuition, room, board, and other requirements, most of which can vary tremendously from school to school. Such factors as the availability of free or low-cost housing, even if that requires living at home, can help you get an education from which you can benefit the rest of your life. You may, alternatively, be able to attend a program that allows you to continue to work. Sometimes postponing your education until you have saved up enough money to go to school may make sense, although the cost of your education may increase at a faster rate than your savings. You must compute the projected cost of your education, then decide what compromises you are willing to accept to reach your goals.

You need to make a realistic estimate of how much your education will cost at each school you are considering, how much you and your family can contribute, and how much you need to seek from outside sources.

Once you have estimated what costs you will incur and how much money you can contribute yourself or obtain from family and other friendly sources, you will have a good idea of about how much money you need to obtain through financial-aid programs. You should try to come up with a reasonably accurate figure that represents the minimum amount of money that will ensure your survival as a student. If you apply for financial aid that is based on need, you have to go through this type of exercise anyway. Putting the figures together in advance will also prepare you for filling out the financial-aid applications and for requesting realistic sums of support.

You can probably expect to earn money working while you are a student, and you should try to estimate how much you might earn as part of your financial planning.

You should also try, perhaps with a little help from students already in the type of program you want to attend, to estimate your potential for earning money while you are a student. If you can work part-time or in the summers, you will be able to make a significant contribution to your education, you will be beholden to no one, you may gain valuable experience, and you will further decrease the amount of money you need to obtain from financial-aid sources.

You will probably have to find some outside sources of support—these change a lot in terms of eligibility, requirements, benefits, and limitations, and you must carefully investigate all options.

In the final analysis you will probably have to seek some money from outside sources, such as governmental programs and the schools themselves. There may be numerous sources of support available to you, but the aid programs can change from year to year and are different from field to field. In all, eligibility for assistance depends on a variety of sometimes complex factors.

The advice provided here is designed to give you some framework for pursuing possible sources of funds. However, the changing nature of the aid programs, the tremendous variability among schools, and the importance of individual factors mean that you must take the initiative and find out exactly what you are eligible for, how to get it, and how to keep it while you are in school. The advice contained in this book is invaluable, but your own efforts are also essential. There is no one who will work as hard for your cause as you can, should, and will be expected to.

If you are eligible, the Veterans Administration provides some of the most generous educational benefits available.

Among the most generous sources of financial aid are the programs designed to facilitate the education and advancement of veterans. Many Americans have received educational support through the Veterans Administration (VA). One of the advantages of the VA program is that many, if not most, universities are not only geared up for accepting veterans benefits, but also have staff members whose sole purpose is to help veterans take full advantage of these programs. In the relatively impersonal atmosphere of higher education there is nothing finer than having an office and staff devoted to your cause. In addition, there are Veterans Administration offices throughout the country that are staffed with specialists in eligibility and benefit determination; they can tell you what funds you can obtain through this source.

Veterans' benefits are generally available to anyone who has served in the armed forces and who meets certain eligibility criteria. These criteria are available from your local VA office and from many of the campus student aid or veterans assistance offices. You can obtain this information, and should do so regardless of what benefits you may think you are eligible for, at any time—you need not have submitted applications for admission or financial aid first. In addition to veterans, certain dependents of veterans may also be eligible for benefits, primarily relatives of deceased, disabled, or missing-in-action veterans where the loss is service connected. You can find out if you are eligible for these benefits through the same channels as a veteran would use.

While Veterans Administration benefits are relatively generous, the exact type and amount of benefits for which you are eligible will depend on a number of factors related to your service record, your prior use of benefits, and the type of educational program you will be enrolled in. Full-time or part-time program status may also affect your benefits.

There may be additional academic requirements of which you should be aware, and you may have to continue to meet certain requirements while you are in training. Thus, your eligibility or support levels may change while you are a student if, for example, you decrease your course load. You should know about these requirements and any changes that could occur in your benefits. You may be eligible for valuable additional benefits, such as tutoring support, which you will also want to find out about. Remember that veterans' benefits are an entitlement program, which means that if you qualify you get the assistance, subject to certain guidelines. And the benefits for which you are eligible will depend on when and how long you served, when you were discharged, and other factors.

There are some important and potentially serious limits to veterans' benefits.

Graduate and professional students interested in veterans' benefits may face some serious barriers. Many entitlement programs have time limits, both in terms of period of eligibility and length of time support can be maintained. Thus you must use benefits within a specified period of time, such as ten years from the date of your discharge. Since graduate education is undertaken after the completion of undergraduate education, and often after you have been out in the working world for a while, the time period of eligibility may expire before you begin or end your training. This is an important consideration in both the timing of your education and your need to assess carefully your individual situation.

Many financial-aid programs, including those of the Veterans Administration, have limitations on how long you can draw benefits.

A second constraint may be even more serious. Many people will use up the number of years of educational support for which they are eligible while in undergraduate education, and by the time they reach the graduate or professional level, they find that they are no longer able to obtain benefits. There is little you can do about this if you need assistance at the undergraduate level. However, recognize that many programs allow you to draw benefits for only a certain number of years and that you must ration these benefit years among your various educational programs. In some instances attendance at a lower-cost college for undergraduate education, without your having to use benefits, may be worthwhile in order to have those benefits available for potentially more expensive advanced education later on. These are extremely complex issues that require a degree of advance planning that is difficult for even the most organized students.

Social security benefits have, in the past, also been available under certain circumstances to students. But these programs are being phased out. This program had been primarily oriented toward undergraduates whose parents were dead, disabled, or retired.

There are financial-aid programs available in virtually every state—but they are usually available only to state residents and may have additional eligibility requirements and benefit limitations.

Most states also have financial-aid programs; these frequently parallel the federal assistance programs. These programs usually require that you be a resident of the state, and there may be additional requirements about where you attend school. Many of these programs also require that you demonstrate financial need. State programs are as complex, by and large, as the federal programs and require homework on your part to figure them out and determine your eligibility.

You need to find out about state programs as part of your thinking about which school to attend and where to apply. Investigation of these sources of support is easily accomplished, either through state offices of financial aid or by contacting local universities—especially state universities. Again, some homework on your part, even before applying anywhere, can pay off later on. The complexities of applying and of eligibility and benefit determination do require some careful investigation. Do not leave anything to chance.

The best bargains in higher education, and of more importance to many students than grant and loan programs, are state universities.

While there are many state grant and loan programs for assisting students, the most important form of assistance is state sponsorship of higher education itself, which usually results in universities with relatively low tuition and fees for state residents. This subsidy is indeed a very generous source of help for students throughout the nation. Other financial-aid programs are available in most states for students with financial need, for certain types of training the state wants to promote, and for minorities and other special categories of students, such as the handicapped. There are many programs, and they vary widely from state to state, although many programs are being reduced due to budget constraints.

Some states have special programs to assist state residents in obtaining training in selected fields in other states.

In addition to providing support for residents studying in their own state, some states also have special programs that provide financial assistance, especially for tuition and fees, for residents to study in other states. This is done when the sponsoring state does not offer state-supported education in a specific field, but wants residents to be able to obtain an education in those fields. The state will then pay for the education of students in other states that do offer that type of training. In most situations there are limitations over who is eligible to participate, where the training can occur, and what fields of study are covered. However, this type of support is frequently available for graduate and professional training, and therefore is very worthwhile checking out. These programs can also be very generous from the student's perspective, paying most costs. But sometimes they only pay the difference between in-state and out-of-state tuition at the guest school. Your eligibility for these programs may also be a factor in the admissions decision.

You should consider declaring your financial independence from your parents, but doing so can have important implications.

Since graduate and professional students are usually older than the typical undergraduate, you should also explore whether or not to declare your own independence for purposes of seeking financial aid. It is very important to determine whether it is to your benefit to be a dependent of your parents. If you are, they can claim you as a dependent on their income tax returns and, in turn, are expected to contribute to your educational expenses. On the other hand, if you can demonstrate your financial independence from your parents, they will not be expected to help you out, and their income and assets will not be used in computing your available resources for financing your education in those assistance programs that require evidence of need. This is another area that can be very complex; you will want to investigate the situation, talk to financial-aid advisers, and maybe even talk to an accountant. There are also legal implications involved in misrepresenting your situation.

Many schools have tuition-waiver or -reduction programs for needy, minority, or university-employed students.

A number of state-supported schools, and even some private schools, also have tuition-waiver programs, often designed for minority students or the very needy. Under these programs either students are not required to pay any tuition or the tuition payment is reduced. In some schools students who are employed as teaching or research assistants may also be eligible for tuition waiver. Spouses of university employees may also be eligible for tuition waiver or reduction. Sometimes eligible students are allowed to pay tuition on an installment plan.

Many employers offer generous educational benefits that pay tuition and other costs and sometimes provide leave with or without pay, but there may be some very significant strings attached.

There are a number of other important sources of financial aid that are in the form of grants that do not have to be repaid in cash. (Obviously grants are usually preferable to loans, which have to be repaid.) Perhaps one of the most important sources of financial aid is employer-sponsored tuition- and expenses-reimbursement programs. Eligibility for these programs is usually dependent on your employment situation and may require that you continue to work at least part-time. Other programs provide from partial to complete educational benefits and sometimes even a leave of absence. And in some instances the employer will even pay part or all of your salary while you are away at school.

A few cautionary notes are in order, however. First, many employers require a commitment on the part of the employee to maintain employment for a specified period of time after benefits are accepted, especially when a leave of absence with pay is granted. If there are any such requirements, you must be willing to meet them.

Second, while you are away from work studying, either full-time or part-time, you may be losing seniority and you may have some difficulty keeping up with the politics of your workplace. Remember to plan for reentry after your education so that you will not be penalized even indirectly for having been away. On the other hand, the short-term costs may be minor compared with your long-term gain from your new education. Again, the trade-offs are very complex.

Some employers offer educational benefits for spouses and children of employees.

In some instances the children of employees may be eligible for educational grants or scholarships, so you may want to check with your parents' employers concerning your own eligibility for assistance. A spouse may also be eligible for some benefits. Sometimes an employee with clout can negotiate educational benefits for his or her children or spouse as an additional employee benefit, one that can have a lot of value. Many companies have specific programs for providing scholarships to the children of employees. These may be either entitlement or competitive programs based on scholastic achievement.

Many federal and state grant and loan programs face reductions, elimination, or eligibility restrictions, while others have always been available only to selected students.

Only a minority of students will be able to take advantage of such programs as employer-paid benefits. Most students will have to rely on other sources of support, such as federal government grants and loans. Unfortunately, not only are many federal grant programs being reduced or eliminated, but some of the major grant programs are not available for study beyond the bachelor's degree. Some state programs that are tied into the federal programs are also restricted to undergraduate education. And some grant programs have extremely restricted eligibility, such as those administered by the U.S. Bureau of Indian Affairs, which are available only to Native Americans, Eskimos, and Aleuts. If you fall into these categories, you should check on the extent to which you are eligible for financial assistance through any office of the Bureau, university financial-aid offices, or your usual source of assistance information.

A number of federal and state grant programs are available for certain individuals who meet specific eligibility criteria. For example, in many states there are special assistance programs available for the dependents or spouses of policemen and firemen and certain others who have been totally disabled or killed in the line of duty. Other programs exist to aid the handicapped and other individuals with special needs.

Grant and loan programs have been available in specific professions where there has been a personnel shortage, but these programs are also subject to change on relatively short notice.

There has also been a wide range of grant programs for students in specific fields of study. These programs, mostly funded by the federal government, were developed for the purpose of increasing the number of professionals in certain "shortage" fields in the United States. Some states have also developed programs in selected fields for the same purpose. The fields covered by these programs have included bilingual education, nursing and other allied health-care professions, health services administration, and others.

However, due to rapidly changing federal directions and limitations on state resources, combined with the recognition that some of these professions are no longer in a situation of severe national shortage, there have been significant changes in the aid that is available and in the design of the programs themselves. There is one excellent source of information about these financial-aid programs, however, and that is the program or programs to which you are applying. You can find out if there is a grant program in your field by contacting any reputable program. The program faculty and staff will be very aware of the current situation, of what funds are available, and of what the eligibility requirements are.

Not every program is eligible to have its students receive federal- or state-sponsored training support.

However, be aware that not all graduate and professional programs are eligible for this financial assistance, even if money is currently available from federal or state resources. There are usually guidelines that require that a school's educational program meet certain specific criteria, such as some form of national accreditation, before they are authorized to accept and distribute grant funds. And even then they may have other requirements placed on them that limit which students in the program can be awarded funds. For example, funds may have to be awarded on the basis of financial need or other criteria. Furthermore, the program may not be required to distribute funds to every student who requests them. As a result, you should check out the situation in your intended field of study and determine what funds are available, how they are distributed, and what the policies are of each of the programs to which you may apply.

You may be able to obtain free or low-cost training if you agree to pay back an employer or the government through subsequent service.

In addition to outright federal subsidies through grants and traineeships, in some fields there are also opportunities for support from the federal government in exchange for subsequent service to the country. Again, the benefits of and eligibility for these programs frequently change over time, and the programs may be eliminated or expanded on relatively short notice.

In medicine, dentistry, and certain other fields, there have been federal programs that pay tuition and sometimes living expenses in exchange for an agreement to serve in an area of the country with a shortage of professionals. Where these programs are still available, you may be required to work in federal service or in another organization under a federal contract.

The military, including the National Guard, probably sponsors more students in more fields than any other employer and is likely to continue to do so. The ultimate such sponsorship is probably the military services medical school located outside of Washington, D.C., where you can receive a free medical education while on federal salary in return for a certain number of years of service as a military physician after training. However, this is such a good deal that admission is extremely competitive.

Grants are better than loans, but loans can make your education happen—just keep your eyes open and read the fine print.

Obviously it is better to get a grant, which does not have to be paid back, than to have to resort to a loan. However, loans may pay for themselves if your education opens the door to professional and financial success. There are many loan options that you can consider. But remember that a loan has to be paid back, and you should never accept so many loans that they become a crippling burden to you after you graduate. Some loans may even have requirements that you start repaying them before you graduate, or immediately after you graduate, regardless of whether you have a job. Some loans may have relatively high interest rates, while others may be subsidized by the federal or state government.

Since loans have to be paid back, they may be a significant burden for you for many years after you graduate, and may require that you forgo some other spending or savings plans. You should understand these commitments before you accept the loan, not after you have to start paying back the money you owe.

The best source of loans for you may be family or friends. You may be able to negotiate a loan with your parents or with a wealthy relative that is more flexible than a bank loan when it comes to repayment schedules, interest rates, and so forth. There are some complex arrangements whereby your parents can loan you large amounts such that you can use the interest that is earned by the loan, but the original loan amount reverts to your parents after you complete your education. These arrangements may have tax advantages for your parents but are highly complex and require professional legal and accounting advice.

There are loans available from many governmental and nongovernmental sources, but these options change over time and require advance planning.

Federal and state loan programs for education, such as the National Direct Student Loan Program, a subsidized program for which graduate students are eligible under certain conditions, have been expanded over the years in terms of eligibility and benefits. However, these programs are also changing, and it is essential to inquire about their current status, your eligibility, and the availability of funds for graduate and professional education. The financial-aid office of any major university can provide you with this information very quickly. Unfortunately, any governmental program can change with relatively little notice, and if you are planning on more than one year of education, the ground rules for financial assistance can be very different after you are into your program than they were when you started to consider applying. Thus, you would be well advised to ask the financial-aid specialists what they see coming down the line for the next couple of years in all of the aid programs for which you might be eligible. A little educated guessing will go a long way toward avoiding some rather rude shocks after you are a student and have begun to progress toward your educational goal.

Loans may also be available from banks or other financial institutions, with or without governmental guarantees of repayment. The Auxiliary Loans to Students federal program is designed to facilitate loans from financial institutions for graduate education, but at relatively high cost. In addition, you may be able to borrow directly yourself. If you have worked for a number of years and have established credit, you may be able to take out a loan for educational purposes. If you own a house, you may be able to borrow against that or other assets. Your parents may be able to cosign for a loan with you. You should, however, check out the interest rates, any loan origination or other fees, the other stipulations associated with the loan, and the amount and time periods for repayment. Loans can be a very significant burden for a recent graduate, and you should enter into any such agreement with your eyes open about the consequences.

Minority group members may be eligible for special loan or grant programs sponsored by federal and state governments and by the universities themselves. Additional financial aid for minorities may be available to meet specific needs such as books, tuition, and tutoring or counseling. Campus minority-affairs and financial-aid offices can tell you about available options. There are a number of national foundations that sponsor grant and loan programs for certain minorities, often for training in specific fields such as medicine.

Loans can be a severe burden after you graduate and should be a source of funding for your education only when other sources are inadequate to meet costs.

Loans can be a great burden and are certainly not as desirable as grants. Every effort should be directed toward restraining yourself on the expense side to reduce the need for loans. All other sources of financial aid should be explored and exploited before taking out a loan. When a loan is necessary, you should take advantage of the loan program offering the best terms. And you will want to consider any programs under which loans will be forgiven in return for service. On the other hand, if taking out a loan means that you will be able to obtain your education, or will make the difference between attending an outstanding rather than a mediocre school, you should consider your long-term personal and professional goals first.

Many scholarships are available for students in certain fields or with specific qualifications.

Scholarships and other special awards are available in an amazing number of fields. Often these awards are for small amounts, and many require financial need. But some are based solely on scholarship or professional promise, and many also represent an honor for the recipient, thus contributing more than just financial resources to the student who wants to accumulate an impressive record. Many scholarships and awards are designed to honor outstanding students in specific fields.

Some are available to individuals with certain qualifications, such as religious affiliation, special abilities, or affiliations with specific companies, unions, or service organizations. The financial-aid office of the university and, more importantly, the program you want to attend will know about these opportunities. Usually you have to apply to each separately, and frequently a letter of endorsement from the program faculty will be required. Professionally oriented awards, which may require an essay or other statement from you, may be available from organizations that are as far-ranging as professional women's groups, which honor the potentially high achievement of female students, or scientific agencies, which support promising young researchers.

Some scholarships and fellowships, which can be substantial, are funded by the federal government for training scientists and certain other types of professionals. Major national competitions may be involved in these programs, and early application may be necessary. You should not wait too long to check out the possibilities. Some financial-aid programs may even require that you apply before you are accepted into a school, with the award being contingent on your acceptance.

Many universities themselves have scholarships available through gifts they receive or as the result of using endowment and other income for this purpose. Sometimes much of this money is directed toward undergraduate students. However, each university that you apply to will be able to tell you what financial aid is available from their own resources.

You can earn money through a number of work possibilities, including work-study.

In addition to grants, loans, and scholarships, there are a number of work opportunities designed to assist you. These are in addition to those discussed in the previous chapter. The most important work program for college students has probably been the federally subsidized work-study program. You can work in a qualified agency, including the university, and be paid in part by governmental and in part by agency resources. This program, like all governmentally sponsored programs, is subject to change, cutbacks, or elimination. Work-study jobs, if available in your areas of professional interest, may also provide you with a chance to gain some valuable experience. More extensive work programs, such as cooperative education, may also be available.

Many professional and graduate programs have other work opportunities available, such as assistantships and working for faculty members on their research, consulting, and service activities. The more professionally active your faculty, the more options that are likely to be available to you.

There is no one source of financial-aid information, and you will have to do some digging.

Unfortunately, there is no one source of financial aid or even one place to obtain all of the information that you need to identify the assistance for which you are eligible. You will need to do a lot of digging yourself. You can contact the financial-aid office of a nearby but relatively large university to find out what sources of support are generally available for graduate students with your background. Usually these offices are staffed by experts who have a lot of information available to them. They may also be able to give you booklets, application forms, financial-aid statements, and the like. Recognize, however, that state programs vary widely, and you will have to obtain information from a university in the state in which you have eligibility, which may be your state of residence, the state in which you will likely attend school, or both.

The specific options available in your field of study may only be known to the program officials themselves. Any major program in your field should have general information on what options are available to students who study in those programs. This will give you some background information.

Specific information on exactly what sources of assistance you are eligible for must be obtained from those programs and universities that you are considering attending. In the final analysis you probably won't be able to find out about all of the sources of support that are available until you are accepted into a program and can work with one specific program office. Many sources of support are unique to those individual programs which have cultivated certain benefactors over time.

Most academic program offices and faculty aren't interested in spending a lot of time helping you obtain financial aid.

The program that you apply to may not be enthusiastic about helping you find out about all of the potential sources of financial aid. There is no one source of assistance, and there are numerous avenues that must be pursued by each student. An incredible amount of effort can go into identifying all of these sources for each applicant, and few programs can put forth such an effort for everyone who applies. Even after you are accepted, the burden of finding out about all of these sources and types of assistance, and for making most of the decisions, will be on your shoulders.

Do not badger the program office about financial aid. You will often find that they are not the experts you might have expected them to be; but they can usually direct you to other experts, such as the financial-aid office, and will probably have some information, especially about assistance available only to students in your field of study. They probably don't even list all of the scholarships and awards that there are, nor will they be likely to give you a lot of generic information that applies to all graduate students; this is available from the financial-aid office.

Financing Your Education: Sources of Funds

University experts in financial aid, given the complexity and changing nature of assistance programs, are important sources of information. If your program is very large, there may be a financial-aid office within the program office itself. Otherwise you will need to find out where to obtain information relevant to graduate and professional study, which can differ significantly from undergraduate educational assistance.

Finally, don't expect a lot of assistance from the program faculty. Most of them know little about financial aid, really don't care, and are likely to be irritated with such questions. They will help you in securing employment, in writing letters of endorsement, and the like after you are in the program.

Financial-aid application forms must be properly completed, and deadlines must be followed; all procedural aspects of seeking assistance require considerable diligence.

There are many important procedural considerations in obtaining financial aid. Since you may have to apply to multiple sources of assistance, you will have to complete many forms on schedule. Financial-aid deadlines are often very rigid, and you must observe them.

After you determine the assistance programs for which you are eligible, you will have to obtain the appropriate instructions, application forms, and so forth. Each application, each deadline, and each requirement must be observed and followed. This is your responsibility. Some sources of support will not be available to you until you have been admitted into your program, and sometimes not even until you have completed one or more terms. Be aware of all eligibility requirements and other essential guidelines associated with each of the assistance plans you are interested in pursuing. If you are a member of a minority, visit the minority-affairs office on campus to get advice and assistance.

If you are awarded financial aid, it is also your responsibility to let the agency or office that issued the award know whether you accept and other details of your educational plans; the award may also require renewal in subsequent years.

As with the admissions decision, if you receive an award, you should indicate to the granting agency whether or not you accept it, what your specific plans are, and any other information that they require. Since the award to you may be at someone else's expense, you should reply as soon as possible, especially if you are going to decline the offer, so that the money can either be allocated to you or offered to others.

Many financial-aid awards are not automatically renewed for subsequent years. If your education requires more than one year of support, and in some instances even more than one term, you may need to reapply for additional aid. This again is your responsibility and is obviously important to do. Sometimes interim reports of your progress may be required from you or the school, and you should be sure that all such requirements are met.

There are many ways to pay for an education; you need to decide which will work best for you and what compromises you are willing to accept.

When you look at the overall picture, which this and the preceding chapter have tried to help you do, there are many financing options available to graduate and professional students. These options include much more than just grant and loan programs. The entire design of your strategy for selecting programs and schools, for applying to programs, and for making your final selection should consider the financial aspects of your education. You may want to work harder at gaining admission to specific programs so as to reduce the costs or

Financing Your Education: Sources of Funds

increase the value of the education you receive. You will want to look at the expense side of your education as carefully as the revenue side.

There will always be ways to finance an education. What should be especially important to you is to consider the trade-offs you are willing to make: costs versus quality; costs versus location; living at home versus living away; loans versus grants; working versus not working; and so forth. These are difficult issues to consider and complex alternatives to weigh. But they are obviously integral to your admissions strategies and to the course of your career.

There are some other ways to obtain support which may also be worthwhile considering.

In addition to the more traditional sources of financial aid, you may want to consider some more unusual approaches. In some states, depending on your family and personal situation, you may be eligible for social welfare programs, such as Aid to Families with Dependent Children. If your education results in your eventually becoming a wage-earning taxpayer, the costs to the state may be well worth the investment of support while you are in school.

Sometimes there are professional contests that can result in some financial aid. These might include essay contests or other types of student competition. Even if there is relatively little money involved, every little bit helps, and there are some professional-development benefits as well. Oftentimes these types of opportunities, and many others, become available once you are in a professional or graduate program.

Most forms of financial aid are awarded either when you are admitted or report for the start of the term. This can increase your uncertainty, since you may not know how much financial aid you will be able to obtain until after you have to make a decision. This inherent uncertainty may be difficult to deal with, but you have to use your best estimates of what will be available to you, perhaps including preliminary commitments. Appendix B is designed to help you with these computations.

When making financial-aid decisions, remember that education is your primary goal, and set your priorities to achieve this result.

In the final analysis people seem to work things out so that they can reach their educational goals. You probably will also. But keep your goals high, and put as much effort as possible into facilitating the achievement of these goals without giving up in the face of what might appear to be insurmountable financial barriers; these barriers can often be brought down, or at least lowered enough to allow you to pass through and reach your own personal goals. That is what you are really striving for in working so hard to gain admission and to find sources of financing for your education.

PART V *Ready to Act*

CHAPTER 17 *Formulating Your Strategies*

THE ORGANIZED AND CAREFUL APPLICANT is the one who is most likely to be accepted. Each chapter of this book deals with a different aspect of the admissions and financial-aid processes and provides clues about how you can improve your chances of admission and of financing your education. However, there are a number of themes that transcend all of the chapters.

The first of these themes is that you should take an analytical approach to the admissions and financial-aid processes. You should carefully think through all aspects of the admissions process and of your decision to seek advanced training. By doing so you can determine how to strengthen your credentials and how to present the strongest possible case to the admissions committee. You should assess your financial needs and all opportunities for obtaining funds.

Second, you should be careful, even meticulous, in complying with all of the requirements for admission and for financial aid, for meeting timetables, and for providing, in the best possible light, all of the information requested of you. A careful, thoughtful approach to admissions and financial aid can be very beneficial.

Third, you must spend the necessary time to understand the nature of the program to which you are applying and to relate the program to your personal and career objectives. This is very important, not only in the admissions process, but also in ensuring that you make the right decision in committing one or more years of your life and considerable money to more schooling.

Each aspect of the admissions and financial-aid processes is important. Each requirement must be given proper attention. You owe it to yourself, and to the programs to which you are applying, to spend the time and effort needed to present yourself as favorably as possible.

You would be wise to take a strategic planning approach. Lay out in your mind, and perhaps even on paper, what your goals are and how you will achieve them. Outline how each of the programs to which you are applying will help you meet your goals. Then list each of the credentials that are necessary to gain admission. List your own strengths and weaknesses and how you can best present yourself. As you complete each of the requirements for application, check them off your list. Assess the financial costs of each program, and think about these costs in light of the quality and value of the education that you will receive.

Appendix A is designed to help you get started on the formulation of your strategies. Fill in the items on the table as they relate to your own credentials. Then obtain the comparable information from each of the programs to which you are thinking of applying. Determine how you stand in comparison to the students who have been accepted in past years. This is a starting point for assessing your strengths and weaknesses. You can also use this information to determine what attributes you must emphasize and which weaknesses you must play down. In completing the table in Appendix A, add any additional items that may be relevant to the admissions decision. Refer to the other chapters of this book to help you interpret how you stand and how you might improve your chances of admission.

Earlier chapters have recommended that you avail yourself

of the free counseling that is widely offered. This advice cannot be emphasized enough in terms of both admissions and financial aid. Practitioners, college advisers, and the programs themselves are all sources of valuable information. The more information and knowledge that you have about the field of practice and the admissions process, the better able you will be to improve your chances of admission. And the more information you have, the better able you will be to make correct and appropriate career decisions, to defend those decisions to the admissions committee, and to line up financing.

This book is written to provide "generic" advice to individuals seeking admission to, and financing for, a multitude of different programs. Each field—indeed, each program—has its own unique characteristics, but most share a common set of basic principles. Appendix C provides a glossary of terminology to aid you in understanding these principles and the language used in this book.

The best sources of information about individual programs are the programs themselves. Remarkably, most programs will provide a large volume of free information to potential students. You only need to write a brief letter or postcard—or even stop by the program office, if that is convenient—to obtain this free information. By examining information from eight or ten programs, you will gain considerable insight into the admissions processes, financing opportunities, and decision criteria that are commonly used in your chosen field.

Once you have assembled and assessed this information, you are ready to begin the application process. The chapters of this book tell you how to facilitate that process and how to improve your chances of admission by presenting the best possible credentials. How carefully you do so is up to you. The time and effort you expand on the admissions effort is also up to you.

The importance of presenting the best possible credentials to the admissions committee cannot be stressed enough. Hindsight after rejection will do little to bolster the spirits of a rejected applicant. Spending the time to prepare the best possible application is something that should be at the top of your list of priorities. Careful consideration of each aspect of the application process can pay off. Why take a chance?

Successful applicants will have their work cut out for them. Some people will be accepted on a contingency that requires them to complete additional coursework or do something else to strengthen their credentials. These contingencies are due to a desire to ensure that each student is as well prepared as possible for the rigors of advanced study—they are not just more hoops to jump through. All applicants have to decide if they have the commitment and stamina needed to survive the demands of the program. After acceptance the real work begins.

Success in applying to, and obtaining funding for, graduate or professional school requires the same commitment and hard work as success in other activities in life. There are shortcuts, and there are people who are sloppy and take a lackadaisical approach who nevertheless gain admission. But for most applicants a little extra care and consideration can enhance the chances of admission. Isn't that a small price to pay when your future is at stake?

Appendixes

APPENDIX A *Personal Assessment Table*

THE TABLE on the following pages should be utilized to assess your attributes and to compare your credentials with those sought by the schools and programs to which you are applying. Obtain information from the programs where possible, and assemble the information on your own credentials, so that you can determine your strengths and weaknesses. A careful and critical evaluation of your record will be conducted by the admissions committee. It would be best if you do this yourself first, so that you can determine how you are likely to fare and which of your attributes should be emphasized when applying. This is a time for honesty and openness. Critical self-appraisal is never easy, but it can be most valuable.

The table should be completed as follows:

1. Place your name at the top.
2. List each program on the line at the top; use additional sheets to include more programs.
3. For each admissions criterion listed in column 1, list your credentials in column 2.
4. For the standardized tests, adapt the table to the test or tests that are required for the programs to which you are applying. Most tests have different sections for which scores are separately reported. List these individually

Personal Assessment of Application Credentials for _____
(Insert Your Name)

Admissions Criteria	Your Credentials	Admission Requirements for Programs: (Insert Name of Each Program)
(1)	(2)	
Grade-Point Average: —Overall —Last Two Years —Specific Courses		
Standardized Test Scores: —Overall —Part A: —Part B: —Part C: —Part D: —Part E:		
Motivation: Rating: High, Medium, Low		

Personal Assessment Table

Personal Assessment of Application Credentials for _____
(Insert Your Name)

Admissions Criteria	Your Credentials	Admission Requirements for Programs: (Insert Name of Each Program)
(1)	(2)	
Undergraduate Major:		
Prior Graduate Degrees:		
Letters of Reference: —Number, Quality		
Experience: —Years Overall —Years in Field		

Appendix A

Personal Assessment of Application Credentials for _____
(Insert Your Name)

Admissions Criteria	Your Credentials	Admission Requirements for Programs:
(1)		
(2)		
Prerequisite Courses:		
Other Criteria (list each):		

under Part A, Part B, etc., for as many parts as are necessary.
5. List your personal motivation as high, medium, or low.
6. Complete the rest of the credentials, and add any that are known to be required (for example, the completion of prerequisite courses such as organic chemistry).
7. Enter the program admission requirement for each criterion under the appropriate program. This information should be obtainable from the programs.
8. Critically examine the table, and compare your credentials to the mean or recommended ones for each program, in order to assess your strengths and weaknesses.
9. Rationally formulate your admissions strategies.

APPENDIX B *Financial-Aid Worksheet for Graduate and Professional Students*

(Complete for each year of graduate/professional studies)

Your Name: _____

List Programs You Are Considering:

_____ _____ _____ _____

Expenses Per Year (Estimated):

Tuition

Fees

Room

Food

Books

Entertainment

Transportation

Financial-Aid Worksheet

Other (specify):

_____

_____

_____

_____

_____

_____

TOTAL ESTIMATED EXPENSES
   (should equal total below):

_____

*Revenue and Income
   Per Year (Estimated):*

Parent Contribution

Student's Own Contribution

Spouse Contribution

Summer Employment

School-Year Employment:

   Work-Study

   Assistantships

   Consulting

   Other (specify):

   _____

   _____

Scholarships

Grants

Loans

Other Awards

Other Sources of

  Support (specify):

_____

_____

_____

_____

TOTAL REVENUES AND INCOME
  (should equal total above):

APPENDIX C A Glossary of Admissions and Financial-Aid Terms

Accreditation. National or regional recognition of a program as meeting certain minimum professional training standards.

Admissions committee. Faculty committee in a graduate or professional program that is responsible for determining which applicants are accepted into the program and for related policy and procedures functions.

Auxiliary Loans to Assist Students. Alternative "market" interest-rate loan program requiring higher repayment rates and other more severe constraints than earlier federally sponsored loan programs. Graduate students are eligible.

Credentials. All of the documentation that an applicant submits for consideration by the admissions committee.

Criteria. Factors that are considered for admission, such as grades, standardized test scores, and prior training; standards are associated with specific criteria to define exact levels or values that are required or sought by the program.

Deadlines. Mandatory dates by which admissions and financial-aid requirements must be submitted.

Eligibility. A student's ability to obtain funds through entitlement programs; criteria for eligibility can be based on many different factors.

Entitlement program. Assistance program that is available to all students meeting eligibility criteria; usually government sponsored.

Financial aid. Monetary assistance for students to allow them to obtain further education.

Financial need. Dollar amount that a student needs to obtain from financial-aid sources after determining what can be paid from his or her own resources and those of the family.

Graduate program. Educational training program in an academic field such as the arts, sciences, or liberal arts.

Grant. Financial aid that is awarded and paid without any repayment requirements.

Guaranteed Student Loan Program. Federally sponsored loan program for students with subsidized interest rates; subject to restrictions for eligibility, loan terms, and other aspects of the program; may be reduced or eliminated for graduate and professional students.

Independent student. An individual who is deemed not to be a dependent of his or her parents for purposes of financial-aid eligibility.

Loan. Financial aid that must be repaid and for which interest is usually charged; there are numerous sources of student loans.

Loan forgiveness. Elimination of a previous loan obligation, usually in exchange for some type of service or other commitment.

Matriculation. Registration in a new program or school by a student for the first time.

Minority. Individual with recognized affiliation with one of the nation's traditional minority groups, such as blacks, Spanish-surnamed people, or American Indians; minority definitions can vary depending on the program.

National Direct Student Loan Program. Federally sponsored student loan program with subsidized interest rates, which is locally administered by the university; graduate and professional students have been eligible for this program.

Opportunity costs. Alternatives that a student gives up by going to school; these include employment possibilities.

Private university. Institution of higher education that is not governmentally owned.

Professional goals and strategies. An applicant's long-term career desires, and pathways to achieve those wants.

Professional program. Educational training program in a professional field such as medicine, law, or business.

Program. Educational training unit of a college or university.

A Glossary of Admissions and Financial-Aid Terms

Public university. Institution of higher education that is state-owned and -operated or -affiliated, primarily for state residents.

Qualified minority. Applicant with minority status who meets a program's minimum standards for minority applicants.

Reference. Opinion of an applicant as expressed by a relatively objective reviewer.

Resident tuition. Tuition or fees charged to state residents by state-sponsored universities and colleges.

Scholarship. A grant awarded on the basis of academic or other criteria, not based on financial need; there are many, many sources and types of scholarships.

Social Security educational benefits. Support program under the authority of the Social Security Administration for certain eligible students who were or are dependents of retired, disabled, or deceased beneficiaries; this program is probably going to be phased out completely.

Standards. Specific values that the admissions committee seeks in applicants for each of the admissions criteria; for example, specific required grade-point averages.

Training grants and fellowships. A variety of federal, state, and private grants and scholarships that have been available to certain students in specific fields where there has been a national need for personnel. Specific programs have changed over time and are continually subject to further change and even phase-out. There have been programs in law enforcement, in the health professions, and in education. Some programs have been specifically limited to minorities or women. Many programs have been designed for graduate and professional students. Some of the programs have also included loan programs.

Tuition waiver. Reduction or elimination of a student's tuition-payment obligation.

Veterans' benefits. Assistance programs administered by the Veterans Administration for eligible veterans of the armed forces. Specific eligibility criteria, benefits, and other requirements can be obtained from the VA or campus veterans-assistance office.

Work-study. An employment program oriented toward financial aid for students who qualify in which the employing agency pays part of the costs and the government pays the remainder.

Index

academic awards, admissions selection and, 78
acceptance by school, conditional, 39, 151–155
  additional credentials and, 154
  avoiding requirements imposed in, 153
  "contractual" nature of, 151–152
  mandatory contingencies in, 151, 154–155
  rejecting offer of, 157
  risks implied by conditions in, 153–154
acceptance by student:
  communication with program after, 158–159
  deferred admission and, 159–160
  evaluating multiple offers and, 156–158
  informing rejected program, 158
accredited programs, 22–23
admissions committee decisions, 149–160
  letters of acceptance, 151–153
  notification of, 149–150
  rejections in, 156, 161–166
  rolling admissions and, 32
  special conditions and, 151–155
admissions committees, 7–8, 17
admissions interviews, *see* interviews
admissions process, 3–10, 18–19
  component parts of, 8–9
  instructions for, 5, 9
  structure of, 6–7
Advanced Knowledge Test, 91–92
Aid to Families with Dependent Children, 211
application fees, 28
application process, 29–84
  answering questions for, 40–41
  "brains" vs. maturity and experience in, 98
  career goals and, 15–19, 20
  completion of, 37–38, 39, 50–51
  connections (back-door) and, 42, 129–138
  credentials in, 9–10, 47, 52–89, 217
  difficulties in obtaining records for, 32
  essay questions in, 49–50
  extraneous material in, 99–101
  grades in, 9–10, 66–82, 144–145
  graduate-level performance and, 42, 80
  initiation of, 29–34
  law of diminishing returns of, 27–28
  memberships in honorary societies and, 78
  minorities and, *see* minorities

Index

application process (*continued*)
  narrative or personal statements for, 47–51
  number of schools to contact in, 26–27
  older students and, 98–99
  optional or elective questions in, 41–42
  previous schools listed in, 42–43
  program evaluation and, *see* programs; program selection
  program vs. university-wide forms, 38–39
  redundant information for, 38, 45
  references for, 45, 52–65
  résumés in, 47
  status of college and, 25–26, 67–70
  summarized, 215–218
  supplementary information for, 44–45, 46–47
  test scores and, 9–10, 30, 83–94
  transcripts in, 32
  typing of, 40, 50
  undergraduate courses and, 71–72
  undergraduate majors and, 70–72
  undergraduate programs and, 69–70
  women and, *see* women
  work experience and, 43–45, 95–101
Auxiliary Loan to Students, 204

back-door admissions, 129–138
  donations and, 131–132
  strategies for, 137–138
bilingual education, grants for study of, 200–201
books and supplies, costs of, 176–177

career goals, 15–19, 20
  choosing among admission offers and, 157
  long-term view of, 181
  personal goals and, 15–16
  social commitment and, 18
  specific objectives in, 17
childcare services, 182

colleges and universities, national reputations of, 25–26, 67–70, 157
computer screening, 4
conditional admissions, *see* acceptance by school, conditional
connections, 129–138
  alumni as, 133–134
  current students as, 136–137
  faculty members as, 132–133
  morality of using, 130–131
  politicians as, 135
  relatives as, 42
contacts with schools, 29–34
  first step in, 29–30
  letter requesting information as, 31
  maintaining, 31–32
  post-application, 33–34
"contracts," between students and schools, 151–152
costs, 169–212
  admission offers and, 157
  of application fees, 28
  of books and supplies, 176–177
  bottom-line, 189
  estimating, 170, 176, 191–192
  of housing, 175
  indirect, 11–15, 170, 179–180
  of living expenses, 174–178
  of private vs. public institutions, 24, 171–172, 196–197
  of quality vs. low-cost school, 178
  standard of living and, 11–15, 177–178
  study vs. work considerations and, 185, 187–188
  of transportation, 175–176
  of tuition and fees, 170–174
counseling, guidance, 33, 217
credentials, 9–10, 52–89, 217
  explaining problem areas in, 47
  see also grades; references; standardized tests

deadlines, importance of, 30, 195
deferred admissions, 159–160

Index

directories, of graduate programs, 22
employers, as financial aid source, 198–199
employment:
 through faculty members, 188
 in financing graduate school, 184–188
 "old-boy" and "old-girl" networks and, 20
 seniority in, vs. graduate degree benefits, 180
 for spouse, 181–182
essay questions, in application process, 49–51
experience and background, in admissions selection, 43–45, 95–101

faculty members:
 admissions process and, 4, 5
 back-door admissions and, 132–133
 job opportunities through, 188
 letters of reference from, 55–58
 pre-admission contacts with, 33–34
 as sources of program information, 23, 24
federal grant and loan programs, 200–201
fellowships, 205–206
financial aid application forms, 209
financial aid awards, acceptance of, 210
financial aid experts, as information sources, 208–209
financial aid sources, 190–212
 admission offers and, 157
 Aid to Families with Dependent Children as, 211
 Auxiliary Loan to Students as, 204
 employer educational benefits as, 198–199
 federal programs as, 195–196, 207
 grant and loan programs, restrictions on, 199–200
 grants vs. loans as, 202–203
 information about, 207–209
 loans as, 202–205
 for married women, 148
 military, 202
 National Direct Student Loan Program as, 202–203
 National Guard as, 202
 parents' support as, 182–183, 197–198
 professional training support as, 200–201
 scholarships and fellowships as, 205–206
 social welfare programs as, 211
 spouse's earnings as, 181–182
 state programs as, 195–197
 student's earnings and savings as, 184–188
 time limitations for, 195
 tuition-waiver programs and, 198
 university employment as, 186–187
 Veterans Administration (VA), educational support as, 193–195
 work-study as, 206–207
Financial Aid Worksheet, 226–228
foreign students, 146
 standardized tests for, 94

geographic limitations, in school selection, 25
glossary of admissions and financial aid terms, 229–231
GMAT (Graduate Management Admission Test), 83
grade-point averages, rounding upward of, 45
grades, 9–10, 66–82, 144–145
 absence of, 77–78, 80
 absence of, vs. standardized test scores, 78
 "bad" effects of, 81
 in graduate-level courses, 79–80, 81–82
 importance of, 66–67, 72–77
 "inflation," 75–76
 offsetting poor, 81–82, 86

Graduate Management Admission
  Test (GMAT), 83
Graduate Record Examination
  (GRE), 83, 87
  Advanced Knowledge Test, 91–92
  analytical component of, 89
  grants:
    loans vs., 202–203
    restrictions on, 199–200
    training-program, 200–201
GRE, see Graduate Record
  Examination

handicapped students, interviews for,
  105–106
health care, grants for study of, 200–
  201
honorary societies, 78
housing costs, 175

in-state tuition benefits, 172
interviews, 102–125
  avoidance of, 104–105
  conducted by alumni, 106–107
  content of questions in, 118–123
  dressing for, 114–115
  first impressions and, 115–116
  handicapped applicants and, 105–
    106
  importance of, 109, 111–112, 124–
    125
  local, disadvantage of, 106–108
  poise, tact, and discretion in, 106,
    108–109, 116–119, 124
  preparation for, 112–114
  purpose of, 102–104, 109
  request for, 110–111
  scheduling of, 112
  student's questions at, 112–113
  travel to, 104–105

Law School Admission Test (LSAT),
  83
letters:
  of acceptance, 151–153
  for program information requests,
    31
  of reference, 53–65
  of rejection, 161–162
living expenses, 174–178
loans, 202–205
  auxiliary, to students, 204
  grants vs., 202–203
  National Direct Student, 202–203
  restrictions on, 199–200
LSAT (Law School Admission
  Test), 83

major, undergraduate, 70–72
Medical College Admission Test
  (MCAT), 83
memberships, undergraduate, 78
military, as financial aid source, 202
Miller's Analogy Test, 87
minorities, 139–148
  academic standards and, 143
  admissions standards for, 141–142
  application process and, 41–42
  competition for "qualified," 142–
    143
  definition of, 145–146
  discrimination against, 139–140
  equity with white males and, 147–
    148
  financial aid for, 198, 204–205
  grades vs. test scores for, 144
  preferential treatment for, 140–141
  standardized tests and, 94, 144
  women as, 146

narrative (personal) statements, in
  application process, 47–49
National Direct Student Loan
  Program (NDSL), 202–203
National Guard, as financial aid
  source, 202
non-graded undergraduate schools,
  77–78
"nongrades," on transcripts, 80
nursing, grants for study of, 200–201

older students, admissions selection
  and, 98–99

Index

opportunity costs vs. graduate school, 12, 179

parents, financial aid and, 182–183, 197–198
Personal Assessment Table, 221–225
personal essays, in application process, 47–49
personal goals, 15–17
politicians, as connections, 135
post-doctoral studies, 11–12
practitioners, as sources of program information, 23–24
probationary admission, *see* acceptance by school, conditional
professions, as financial aid source, 200–201
programs:
 accreditation of, 22–23
 selectivity indicators of, 21–22
 sources of information about, 22–24, 157, 217
program selection, 20–27
 career goals and, 15–19, 20, 157–158, 181
 changes in, 80
 national reputation and, 25–26, 67–70, 157
 personal needs and constraints in, 24–25

quantitative data for applications, 66–82

reapplication, benefits of, 164–165
reference, letters of:
 personal vs. on-file, 62–63
 right to review, 63
references, 45, 52–65
 academic, 56–58
 academic ability and, 55
 in application process, 32, 45
 emphasis of, 54
 explaining deficiencies in credentials by, 58–59
 from faculty members, 55–56
 importance of, 52
 negative, 64
 professional, 59–61
 providing forms and information to, 61–62
 selection of, 53–54
 written, 53
rejection, 161–166
 appeals after, 165
 assessment of reasons for, 161–163
 reapplication after, 164–165
 reappraisal after, 166
 reasons for, 163
 waiting lists and, 165
résumés, in application process, 47
rolling admissions, 32

SAT (Standardized Admission Test), 91
savings, in financing education, 184
scholarships, 205–206
social welfare programs, as financial aid source, 211
spouses, as financial aid source, 181–182
Standardized Admission Test (SAT), 91
standardized tests, 83–94
 application procedures and, 9–10, 30
 controversy over, 84
 for foreign students, 94
 minority students and, 94, 144
 objectives of, 87–88
 offsetting low scores on, 92
 preparation courses for, 92–93
 purpose of, 83–84
 reporting multiple results of, 89–91
 retaking, 91–92
standardized test scores:
 low grades and, 86–87
 as measures of intelligence, 87
 percentiles of, 88–89
 as predictors of success, 85–86
state programs, as financial aid source, 195–197

state universities, low cost of, 24, 171–172, 196
status of programs, 25–26, 67–70, 157
strategies, formulating, 215–218
students, as connections, 136–137

Test of English as a Foreign Language (TOEFL), 94
training support, state- or federal-sponsored, 200–201
transcripts, 32, 80
transportation, costs of, 175–176
tuition and fees, 170–174
　establishing residency for in-state, 172
　increases in, 173–174
　out-of-state student, 171
　at private schools, 171, 173
　quality of education and, 173–174
　at state-run schools, 24, 171–172, 196

tuition-waiver programs, 198

university-wide applications, 38–39

Veterans Administration (VA), educational support by, 193–195

waiting lists, 165
women, 139–148
　admission standards for, 146–147
　application process and, 42
　discrimination against, 139–140
　equity with white males and, 147–148
　married, financial aid for, 148
　older, 148
　preferential treatment for, 140–141
work experience, application process and, 43–45, 95–101
work-study, 206–207

About the Author

STEPHEN J. WILLIAMS is Professor and Head of the Division of Health Services Administration, and Head and Director of Admissions of the Graduate Program in Health Services Administration, at the Graduate School of Public Health, San Diego State University, San Diego, California. He was previously Associate Director and Chairman of Admissions in the Graduate Program in Health Services Administration and Planning at the University of Washington, Seattle, Washington. He has also been on the faculty of Harvard University. He holds an undergraduate degree from Carnegie-Mellon University, master's degrees from the Massachusetts Institute of Technology and Harvard University, and a doctorate from Harvard University. He is the author of numerous books and articles in the fields of health services administration and population sciences. Professor Williams is also Series Editor of the Wiley Series in Health Services published by John Wiley and Sons, New York. Dr. Williams lives with his wife and three children in San Diego.